Vikings

A Captivating Guide to the History of the Vikings

(The True and Surprising History of the Vikings & the Most Badass Vikings in History)

Robert McKinney

Published By **Jackson Denver**

Robert McKinney

All Rights Reserved

Vikings: A Captivating Guide to the History of the Vikings (The True and Surprising History of the Vikings & the Most Badass Vikings in History)

ISBN 978-0-9948647-4-1

No part of this guidebook shall be reproduced in any form without permission in writing from the publisher except in the case of brief quotations embodied in critical articles or reviews.

Legal & Disclaimer

The information contained in this book is not designed to replace or take the place of any form of medicine or professional medical advice. The information in this book has been provided for educational & entertainment purposes only.

The information contained in this book has been compiled from sources deemed reliable, and it is accurate to the best of the Author's knowledge; however, the Author cannot guarantee its accuracy and validity and cannot be held liable for any errors or omissions. Changes are periodically made to this book. You must consult your doctor or get professional medical advice before using any of the suggested remedies, techniques, or information in this book.

Upon using the information contained in this book, you agree to hold harmless the Author from and against any damages, costs, and expenses, including any legal fees potentially resulting from the application of any of the information provided by this guide. This disclaimer applies to any damages or injury caused by the use and application, whether directly or indirectly, of any advice or information presented, whether for breach of contract, tort, negligence, personal injury, criminal intent, or under any other cause of action.

You agree to accept all risks of using the information presented inside this book. You need to consult a professional medical practitioner in order to ensure you are both able and healthy enough to participate in this program.

Table Of Contents

Chapter 1: Viking Ship, Viking Ship Museum, Oslo. Photo by Grzegorz Wysocki 1

Chapter 2: Early Raiding 18

Chapter 3: Scotland and Ireland 31

Chapter 4: Mainland Europe 73

Chapter 5: Further West 90

Chapter 6: Who were the Vikings? 103

Chapter 7: Norse Mythology 123

Chapter 8: Ragnarok 136

Chapter 9: What the Norse Mythology Meant to the Vikings 146

Chapter 10: Viking Culture 150

Chapter 11: Notable Viking Sagas and Kings 162

Chapter 12: An Overview of Viking and Norse Mythology 177

Chapter 1: Viking Ship, Viking Ship Museum, Oslo. Photo by Grzegorz Wysocki

There was a long-standing belief it was the case that Vikings were an ocean-based civilization that was derived from the sagas which were first recorded in the years after when the Viking Age was in decline however, evidence of this was discovered through the discovery of vessels from burial mounds at the 19th century. A search in 1867 the southwest of Norway found a boat that was discovered around the year 900 A.D., and 13 years later another was found. The burial was likely for a man who was murdered The collection of buried items and animals was massive. In the grave with the deceased was the ship, 12 dogs, six horses, an eagle and three beds. There were also five smaller boats and shields and other things that were believed to be necessities for the deceased.

The 1904 year saw a further amazing discovery was discovered in the burial site of Slagen in Norway and it was discovered that the Oseberg ship was found. The ship, which was where two women were buried, women, of which one was the slave of another, was conserved and then transported to Bygdoy in the vicinity of Oslo which was rebuilt and displayed alongside two additional Norwegian vessels.

Oseberg Ship

It is believed that the Oseberg ship, which was dated by Dendrochronology (tree rings) from 820 A.D., is 70 feet long with an overall beam of 17 feet. It was a clinker-built boat. The structure of the hull which included stem, keel and stern and was attached by iron nails and 12 overlaid plansks of oak (lap-strake) to each side of the vessel. The stabilizing ribs, the twarts, and the inner keel were put in. This construction method differs from the standard method of placing down the keel, and then attaching the lower ribs prior to attaching the planking of the hull.

The direction of the Oseberg ship was controlled via a rudder on the side facing the stern. The rudder was driven by 30 rowers, who operated the oars, which were made from wood. The work required to place the Oseberg vessel on the burial mound demonstrates how crucial the burial for ships was within Viking society. It was pulled from the sea, and then transported some distance by rollers to the top of the mound. Here it would have been laden with the things needed by women who had died who lived in the ether, like pots, knives as well as beds, woollen blankets and quilts as well as her female slave. In addition, the burial included the carve-out cart, three sledges as well as an oxen saddle along with horses, horses and dogs. Researchers believe that the intricate burial would have lasted around four months.

The clinker-built Viking ship was robust and pliable, and was sealed with wool wool. Thwarts that maintained the stiffness of the hull also functioned as seats for rowers. They provided the sole source of power in the beginning Viking vessels. The time was around 800 when the sail was first introduced and soon was the primary source to power Viking vessels, and one that was mastered by the Vikings with incredible ease.

In the past, Viking vessels were found and not in burial mounds but as wrecks. There was one among these vessels an enormous warship that was discovered in Hedeby harbor in Denmark built around 985. It was destroyed and then sunk more than 25 years after. It was 100 feet long, having a beam of eight feet. It was propelled by 60 oars as well as the large square sail. Given that it stood at a height just 4 feet in the middle It is believed that it was intended for use in the waters that were protected in the coastline of Baltic. Additionally, there were large ships designed for longer open-sea cruises. one was found under the water in the harbor of Roskilde located in Denmark. The particular ship was approximately 100 feet in length, and was built close to Dublin in the year 1042. Another ship from Roskilde was, on the foundation of the remaining parts of the keel, believed to be 120 feet long. Both ships were built with a depth enough to enable vessels to manage the high seas that surrounded the Atlantic.

As they worked on the construction of long vessels as well, the Vikings created a range of specially designed cargo vessels which could be managed by a smaller team. They had just a few rowers for operating in tight areas like rivers. They also had low draughts but could carry tons of goods. The five vessels discovered at Skuldelev in Denmark and measuring 50 feet in length could hold up to 24 tonnes of freight. Through the sailing of a replica of the ship, which was built around 1039 and has been dubbed Skuldelev 1. It is determined that the crew been between seven and five. The increase in the number of effective trade vessels in the Vikings likely resulted from the growing demand of low-cost consumer items in the home in the course of time, Scandinavian society grew more divided and the requirement to offer the transportation of goods between Scandinavia and other distant Viking settlements was growing.

Skuldelev Ship 2

The Vikings were the first to use "dead-reckoning", a method for determining latitude using the help of a sun-shadowed board. A disc that had an axis that could be adjusted to match the season was floating in a pan of water. The sun's noon-time rays will cast shadows over the disc which would be designated for the right latitude. The direction of the disc could be altered according to the relationship to the mark. This easy method for navigation was not often used as Vikings generally conducted their travels on legs, of hopping from one island to the next. Additionally, within the Baltic and North Atlantic, the legs of their voyages were shorter duration. An Viking ship could go between Denmark through Scotland or Norway and back to the Shetlands in less than 24 hours. In Shetlands Shetlands the Vikings continued their voyage toward Ireland beyond the Orkneys as well as The Isle of Man or traversed across the open north Atlantic up to the Faroes before heading up to Iceland and then on towards Greenland as well as North America.

Through their vessels, the Scandinavian traders traded with many regions across Europe as well as the 8th century was a time of numerous tiny trading stations scattered across the coastlines. The buying power of northern Europe allowed for directly traded market between Scandinavia and other regions which opened up opportunities to export their own raw materials as well as trades. One of the most popular things to sell in Scandinavia were furs and slaves which were common for the area, however the further north an animal was from the higher its value was regarded as. The northern traders benefited from this who soon hunted and conducted trade with tribes, nomads, and other people of the north, for the purpose of selling the furs in Europe. Furs from White Polar Bears were respected with great respect and some Norwegian rulers believed that they were a payoff to northern Sami tribe, while others hunting them on their own. Reindeer, bear, Otter and marten were also types of furs used to adorn the Viking traders in wealth.

It also led to Viking Age traders travel further in the north and east seeking more luxurious and unique varieties of fur. It took them through the interior of Russia and the region where many traces of Viking settlements can be discovered.

Also, this time saw increased trade between various kinds of food. Instead of consuming only the food that was available locally and consuming what was grown locally, the Scandinavian people began eating the food produced by others and the majority originated from further away. Similar to this, there are instances of Viking clothing made from silk, or exotic fur and also jewelry made from certain gemstones, which led historians to suppose that the items were exchanged. In the 10th century, it became more popular to trade with items of everyday use, such as the comb and shoes due to the wealth influx which allowed many people to purchase rather than make these items.

Metal items of all kinds, except the iron ones, were valuable, and numerous blades shipped by mail were directly from the Frankish Empire although they weren't supposed to market weapons to foes. Lead, salt, mercury walnut shells, amber pottery, wine and glass are just a few of the rare items imported into Scandinavia from south but more elaborate and attractive crystals, vessels and beads are also being imported to into Orient and Russia.

The items that came out of Scandinavia included primarily animal-based items, such as furs and skins as well as whale bones and walnut tusks however, slavery was also a major source of income as well, both in Scandinavia as well as for traders who traveled to Europe. The records tell the likes of Ottar and Wulfstan Two traders were sailing from Birka, Hedeby and England Their voyages were documented from both sides of ocean. Another route crossed to the Baltic Sea, to a area in Latvia known as Semigallia. Local merchants then transported products up the Dvina River. Dvina that would require a different type of vessel. It was the usual way of trading throughout Europe in which Scandinavian merchants only used across the coastline and they sold their products in large quantities as well as bought new goods and then returned to the ports of Scandinavia.

It was the Viking Age trade networks required numerous middlemen in order to link different lands. Local trade as well as the growth of craftsmanship brought life to towns as well as larger centers of commerce which strengthened the bonds between all the regions. The Viking expeditions' huge amounts of gold and silver that came to Scandinavia was arousing interested merchants and traders who came from far-off lands such as Spanish-Arabs Saxons, Frisians and Slavs who left footprints of products and also traditions in northern. Over 800 Viking Age Arab silver coins have been discovered in Gotland in present-day Sweden which indicates the acclaim of these precious coins. Naturally, little merchants or ships took the route straight from and the Arab Caliphate or Scandinavia however there are evidences from Arabs traveling the route. Most of the time, the coins were likely to be traded numerous times all over Europe as they traveled to the north.

There are more English silver coins have been discovered in Scandinavia more than England in general, which demonstrates the wealth and power of Vikings in this time, which was derived from their skills in trading, but possibly more so through the Vikings who were able to deceive the English seeking riches. The wealthy Vikings had the ability to obtain tons of silver around the globe, through trading, plundering or bribes, gifts as well as tributes. pirates began to frequent the waters of northern Europe, placing pressure on local chiefs and kings to ensure the safety of vessels carrying cargo into their ports. Protection was typically given by groups of interdependent groups who offered to provide it. It created a sense of trust among traders of different backgrounds, allowing for common cultural values and economic systems being created at different locations.

The turbulent 9th century in which trade changed by raiding to large extent, damaged the Carolingian Empire and required greater maintenance and supervision of ports. This is why a lot of trade centers were shut down during the aggressive and violent phase during the Viking raids. The time was when towns such as Kaupung, Hedeby, Ahus, Lund and Birka came to prosper, and trading patterns in both Scandinavia and Europe were subject to major changes over the period of 200 years following the Vikings and their journeys. The unified nature of Scandinavian tribes rendered local conflict difficult and forced northerners to look elsewhere for areas to pillage and loot. In the last days in the Viking Age, these cities began to wane because of the Russian principledom around Kiev. The Russian monarch put a stop to trade routes connecting the Islamic caliphate as well as the Byzantine Empire to Scandinavia and claimed a lot of the wealth and merchandise to himself, directly impacting the lives and economics of the Scandinavian cities of trade.

Although it is true that the Viking Age is mainly remembered for its violence and is often portrayed as so however, the Vikings' impact on the world was positive. Their trade activities boosted the economy of Western Europe, which had been slowed down by the collapse of the Roman Empire. The people who were the victims definitely had a right protest, however it is true that there were, there are two perspectives to this coin.

Chapter 2: Early Raiding

As per The Anglo-Saxon Chronicle, just before the initial major Viking attack during the Viking wars in England, "Danish men" came to the kingdom of King Brihtric in Wessex. Three ships were bringing supplies to Portland Island, and when the royals rode up to welcome the merchants who were expected They were shot dead. In the next few years several sources talk of the king Offa of Mercia as well as Charlemagne taking steps to strengthen coastal defenses the sea-going pagans, possibly in reference towards the Vikings.

Most well-known of the initial raids on foreign targets from Scandinavian Vikings took place in 793 on the east coast of England in the monastic site of Lindisfarne. The incident were recorded by terrified monks and scribes of the monastery. They accurately described the calamity that took place. Based on the Christian religious ecclesiastic Alcuin from York who was alive in the time of the incident, the whole thing was a total surprise. The Church that was St. Cuthbert as "spattered with the blood of priests of God, stripped of all its furnishings, exposed to the plundering of pagans - a place more sacred than any in Britain." The following year, the Vikings according to an old document "ravaged in Northumbria, and plundered Ecgfrith's monastery at Donemuthan," as well as in the year the year 800 "the most impious armies of the pagans cruelly despoiled the church of Hartness and Tynemouth, and returned with (their) plunder to the ships".

The assault at Lindisfarne was, in the perspective of the victims an event that culminated an omen of bad luck coming from God himself, as portrayed within the Anglo-Saxon Chronicle. After the whirlwinds, flashes fire and hunger The heathens gathered to eat, pillage and wreck the Church of God in Lindisfarne. The reason was that they had been sent by God as in a way of punishment by God as a punishment for monks from the monastery must surely have caused a lot of trouble to the God of heaven in this way. The Vikings however, on the other on the other hand, took an empathetic or more practical perspective on the event and explained the incident with a the opposite background. They were aware of the monastery for a long time before pawning the place, including all of its wealth hidden from the world's view, following numerous trade relations to the kingdom of Northumbria in which it was situated. The Vikings recognized that the monastic institution was constructed a long distance from the nearest town of York and chose it because of its numerous weaknesses.

The significant increase in commerce in the region had been a major contributor to the local economy that grew around the monastic site, which made the outpost a very wealthy one. The opportunity was set as a target, and the Vikings were already aware of waiting for tides, making docking simple and also cutting off the monastery from the roads and lands that led to it, which left the monastery without getting help. The site of the monastery was selected, paradoxically, due to the fact that it was isolated and was difficult to get access via land. Any visitor who wanted to go - or loot the monastery could be seen and even heard about prior to their arrival. Nobody in the monastery was aware of a ship coming in shallow waters arriving from afar across the oceans. The element of surprise to be the Vikings characteristic.

It is also noteworthy that this very first major attack of this kind was targeted at the monastery was a factor in their reputation as being cruel and brutal. The monks and priests been through wars and war before, mostly among their kings and their leaders. However, Christian armys usually left their sacred religious and monasteries to themselves and even when they were in hostile territory. The Vikings didn't have any feelings or distrust of God. Christian God but merely desires for the wealth that resided in these houses of worship even though they Vikings could not have realized that, Lindisfarne was located in the heart of the political landscape in the north, and became an important symbol for Christianity throughout England. This was where an exquisite piece of work called that is the Lindisfarne Gospel, had been made hundreds of years before. In leather, and embellished with gems, it became an important piece of art to the world of Anglo-Saxon.

All this was to make Lindisfarne such a sacred place however, all the saints, books and prayers were not enough to help monks who were residing at Lindisfarne monastery, when Vikings were suddenly able to launch an attack. There was a rumor of an attack that were quickly spread and earned the Vikings not only a bad image but also a reputation for being shrewd as they not only struck a church of God and robbed the place, but they even destroyed holy relics and executed monks, and even abducted certain of them to be sold into slaves. There are no eyewitness accounts that remain, and no one knows for certain how accurate the stories are. However, there's a stone within close proximity to the monastery. likely to have been built one year after the attack to commemorate those who died, and shows a violent attack and prayerful monks.

It is believed that the Yorkish monk Alcuin was the one who wrote the documents that were used for looking into the sacks of Lindisfarne although it was not his presence during the incident. He was a strong advocate for strengthening the power of the Church, something that is crucial to bear at the forefront when you read his research. The monk also knew the monks and bishops in the monastery, which made it difficult for him to be impartial. The records of his time contain some serious exaggerations. But even so the story of the Vikings' activities in Lindisfarne 793 stands against the peaceful trade relations. The invaders were the smallest of fleets of three or four vessels that were breakaway from a larger ship that was heading for Scotland in the year. The plundering of Lindisfarne and the raids on Scotland were met with little resistance. Therefore, bands of Vikings continued to return to them over a period of time.

Another attack reported against a monastery located in England occurred in Northumbria just a couple of years later, in 793. The Donemuthan monastery was sacked with the same brutality like Lindisfarne was. Moreover, these Viking groups are believed to be from Norway however certain records speak about them being Danes. Following the two first attacks against both English kingdoms, there's none of the records that mention attacks on England over the span of nearly forty years The general belief is that the Vikings discovered better opportunities for raiding within Scotland and continued to pillage the Hebrides for a couple of years. It's highly likely that the group of Vikings who attacked Scotland were based around Orkney Isles. Orkney Isles, making it more convenient to distribute their attacks and return often. After a short time they shifted their focus to attack Ireland that at the period was marred by political turmoil and couldn't put sufficient for a fight against the raids.

In England the situation slowed down, until a fresh wave of Viking activity began to be observed in the southern part of England and on the Isle of Sheppey. The year 835 was when the Viking phenomenon became a reality and their activities was not limited to regions like the British Isles and Ireland, they began to show up more frequently across the continent and became an issue for those of the Carolingian Empire. The real start of the more than 200 years of Viking raids began with the help of Danes. In the Anglo-Saxon Chronicle tells of raids every year, and it's possible to follow the footprints of the Vikings by examining this meticulous document. Because of the turmoil in politics within both England as well as Frankia numerous other records were compiled at that period, including Vikings in stories.

In the past, attacks were often triggered in areas that bordered two kingdoms However belligerents could be visible from distant locations and the majority of villages were able to prepare the defenses they would have, protect their possessions and flee all non-fighting residents. The Vikings didn't have any way to escape due to their swift moves, and their assaults may have been described as extraordinary fierce simply due to the fact that they were able to surprise their enemies, giving them an edge. It was easy to fight inexperienced farmers and their tactics didn't need the use of a lot of skill. Early Vikings likely weren't particularly proficient with swords or axes and relied more heavily on brute strength rather as opposed to technique. However, techniques would be developed later on when attempts were made to conquer bigger cities. For instance, the famed attack at Paris during which the Vikings used a range various tactics.

The high point of the Viking Age would also be identified by the turmoil in politics after the demise of the Carolingians in France at the end of the 9th century, and the rivalry between English King and his heirs, and still unstabilized Russia in eastern Russia. The Vikings made use of the turmoil to their advantage and certain instances made alliances with rival tribes or chieftains and kings across the continent, in the process of destroying weaker villages or towns left unprotected by the officials. There were rumors of quick loot, easy targets and a spirit of adventure spread quickly across Scandinavia and encouraged the majority of young people to embark for one of the Viking journeys.

The thrill of adventure gets lost in discussions of the causes behind this sudden rout across oceans. However, those who returned Vikings as well as the poems devoted to them did a great job to glorify and endorse these voyages as being better than what the reality of what they were turn out to. A lot of young men were attracted to show their power in battle instead of battling the rough conditions and hostile climate that awaited them in Scandinavia.

Although the source materials are biased, it's certain that they are different attacks and not simply an effective form of trading. The method by which attack was carried out as well as the speed with which they took place as well as the brutal pillaging and looting make these attacks the first of these kind. Historical scholars are able to classify it as being one of the first attacks generally associated with Vikings. After more than a century of accumulation and centralisation riches, sea-faring Scandinavians were aware that they had plenty of merchandise to be plundering all over the coasts of Britain and continental Europe. It was simpler than establishing trade routes that required crews and the capacity to establish a network that could be used to take a portion of earnings. The system was already stable and was built by a group of artisans merchants, sailors the kings and chieftains, but and did not allow new actors on the stage. The reason for this was that the Vikings arrived with guns as well as a desire to pillage and murder. Additionally, their speedy travel across the ocean instead of slowing across terrain gave the locals and monks very little time to plan for a battle in the beginning.

During these initial assaults, they would be attacked in the middle busy lives.

The famous image of the Viking is to a significant extent exaggerated. But when raids began suddenly there were reasons to be scared of the Vikings were, in most cases legitimate. By the time they reached the 8th century clearly changed their conduct.

Chapter 3: Scotland and Ireland

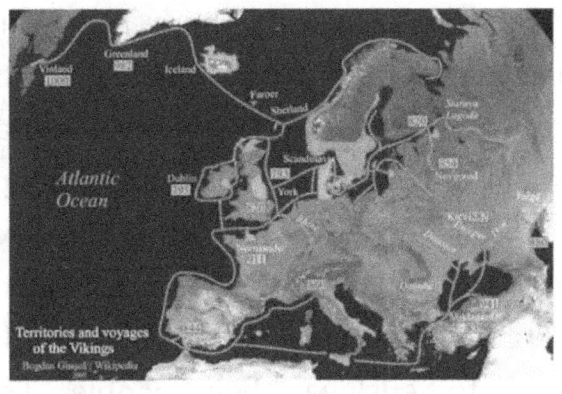

An illustration of Viking fighting throughout Europe

If you read about Viking expeditions in the North Sea and to the west, the focus is usually on the lengthy and exhausting excursions to British kingdoms and on what was happening in the midst of the intrigues and controversies surrounding the English King's such as Ecbert, Aella and Offa. There are more sides of the Vikings who lived in the west and their effect on northern islands that lie off along the coastline of Scotland. There is evidence that Vikings used these islands as their bases to attack Ireland as well as Scotland through the expulsion of the initial people. A number of buildings were destroyed then later adapted to their standards. Ultimately, it's likely the Vikings killed or forced to enslave their people. Local names for locations and landmarks along with the plethora of Viking graves and hoards confirm the full control by Scandinavians within Orkney and Shetland And there's an explanation for why it is believed that the Faroe Islands still belong to Denmark. Nowadays, almost no ancient Pictish names survive however, those with Scandinavian names are commonplace.

The Isle of Man and the Hebrides were colonized by Vikings and the Vikings, however at first, they mostly utilized Orkney and Shetland for attacks against Ireland as well as Scotland. The sources offer a quick outline of the attacks on Iona during 795, 19802 as well as 806, showing the fact that England was left to itself throughout the years, while Vikings were more content to settle in the northern islands, and then launch smaller attacks on islands along the Scottish as well as the Irish coasts. The majority of routes between Orkney and Shetland going west were lined by skerries and islands, which allowed for stopping for supplies, replenish them, or keep out the in the event of bad weather. The journey across Norway to Ireland can therefore be completed very easily during one time as the summer time was spent on islands.

The climate in these regions was in large part like the Scandinavian conditions, which made it easier for Vikings to settle and adapt. However, the main motivations was the numerous abundant and readily accessible resources in the northern regions of England, Scotland, and Ireland and became some of the largest sources of revenue for the Vikings throughout the time. The Orkneys had a significant strategically important position and later became the home of a lengthy family of earls with Norwegian descent but it's unclear the exact date at which it was established. It is generally believed that the islands were occupied in the 8th century towards the end of that is consistent with the time of Scottish as well as Irish raids in addition to the absence of wars on England.

After several years of living on temporary premises after which the Vikings made permanent settlements and built farmlands and villages around the scattered islands on and near the Scottish coast. However, the region remained mostly rural, and the primary commercial centers of the Vikings were Dublin in Ireland as well as York in England and England, which was later taken over by Scandinavians after the Viking Age.

The Vikings' actions in Ireland differed from those they engaged in across Europe as well as the British Isles. Instead of becoming farmers, they went on trading as their primary source of source of income, while also establishing and populating the island. They also served as a kind of mercenaries within Ireland in which the conflicting political factions relied on the skillful Viking warriors, as well as their swift vessels to take with their side during the struggle for power. There were five kingdoms within England in the past and there were more than 150 people in Ireland that were all sovereign, but all belonging to the supreme kings of six with intricate family ties. The country was in the middle of power battles that lasted for a long time, and the Irish conflict was ongoing and intense for quite a duration. The Vikings took advantage of the looting and forced tributes upon several villages and such structures were preserved for a longer period in Ireland rather than other areas of Europe because of the shift in power balances within the region. Norway as well as Iceland could benefit greatly from the Vikings participation in Irish political affairs.

Viking activities within Ireland could be classified into different periods, beginning with 795. It was a short distance prior to the victory over Lindisfarne. Thirty years later, the Vikings had circumnavigated Ireland completely and conducted regular raids against isolated monasteries as well as religious community. They also set a record by petty thefts at the Armagh monastery in Armagh three times within a month in 832. It was likely due to the fact that Armagh was a huge rich and luxurious establishment just a away from the ocean. The majority of the time it was the case that their swift assaults proved successful so it's no wonder that the monks living along the coastline of Ireland were praying for dark nights in order that Vikings could not sail off for sea, like a poem from the same time. Ireland had no major cities during the period, which meant that the sole real source of wealth was in monasteries and churches that served as both political and economic hubs.

These religious objects weren't constructed entirely from precious metals. But they usually had valuable ornaments that Vikings could remove and repurpose into stunning decorations on their own weapons, or even as jewelry to a wife who was lucky. The Vikings were mostly interested in slavery, gold, and honour, just like the other realms they were averse to. The Irish Annals record 26 Viking raids during the first 25 years they were present in Ireland However, at the at the same time, three times the number of violence-instigated attacks were carried out by rival Irish factions. While they were predominantly Christians however, they were not able to give up the church during their battles, because they were also the ones who held the influence of the political and economic authority of the smaller communities in the area at that period. At times, conflicts between two monasteries or between the king and a monastic were fought in Ireland.

At the beginning of the 9th century the Viking presence diminished and the Vikings established a number of ports on the coastline. One of them was Dyflin that translates as "black pool," and it was later changed to an Irish version, Dublin. At this time in time, northern Ireland is still exempt from operations of the remainder of Ireland in addition to the Irish northern kings were able to put up a fight against Viking invasions. In the meantime the there were more Viking raids were conducted and were quickly distributed throughout all of the British Isles and Europe, which left the British as well as the Frankish King in great trouble.

The Viking fleets increased in size and power as they became stronger warriors, better merchants and better tacticians. It happened faster than anyone else in Europe would have expected and made the continent more at risk on numerous areas. In Ireland however it was the case that the Vikings gradually merged and were a blessing to a number of Irish monarchs. In the middle of the 9th century, there were evidence of several marriages in the highest levels of society. Also, the Vikings from Ireland changed their religion to Christianity significantly earlier than people who remained in Scandinavia. It's possible that they embraced the new faith at the beginning of the 10th century. This was before the conversion to Christianity of the different Scandinavians by about one century. This is evidenced by the elaborately decorated graves and crosses, which contain a variety of Christian symbols is used in conjunction with the Runic alphabet. Certain burial crosses also bear designs and pagan symbols that are directly inspired by their Norse mythology. Then there is a new generation of Vikings with Celtic names and inscriptions by rune stones and crosses.

The first Viking runic alphabet contained 24 letters. These letters could be derived from Latin or Etruscan alphabets (which have been modified to eliminate horizontals and curves in order to make them easier to carve into wood or stone). The historians believe that there were experts who were proficient of the alphabet in runes, and these worked for the more wealthy Vikings and royal families in order to make a mark on memorable moments.

Around the middle of the 8th century In the mid-8th century, Vikings ranic alphabet had been reformed to just 16 letters. The runic that was reformed that was referred to as younter futhar each letter was associated with a variety different value of sound. Diacritics later, or accents, were introduced to alter the meaning of specific runic characters. A majority of the 5,000-6,000 runic writings today can be located in Sweden however, an interesting instance is one runic inscription found on the balustrade in Hagia Sophia, a Christian cathedral in Hagia Sophia in Constantinople that is written "Halfdan was here".

It is a Codex Runicus, circa 1300 is among the only a handful of runic textual sources written on parchment. Den Arnamagnaeanske Samling, Copenhagen

The intimate relationship, and subsequent integration can be seen in the remaining images as well as images in tradition of Irish cultural heritage. Ireland was previously not involved in transactions with other nations, and the Viking population was the main factor in Ireland's expansion of trading and exchanges with other countries of Europe. Sea-faring Scandinavians were in close contact with all across the continent. These connections were utilized to create the trade system they constructed upon Ireland.

Following the mighty King Ivar was killed The Vikings were pushed back by the Irish and a lot of them retreated to England as well as Frankia in Frankia, where rampant pillaging was at its highest. But as the violence escalated in the European continent as well as within England The targets gradually began to fight back by removing some Vikings from their new colonies. The result was that they came more frequently in Ireland at the end of the 10th century in search for new opportunities for the island that was previously friendly. Most of them stayed with the practice of constructing ports for trade, that was more suitable than cultivating the squatter soils that dotted the island. It was an effective venture and, under Viking administration, the town of Dublin thrived. Cork, Limerick, Arklow, Wicklow, and Wexford were founded under the same circumstances. They were all founded under similar circumstances. Danish as well as Norwegian Vikings held kingship over Dublin that brought them into the political system of Ireland however, eventually, the Vikings began to split and began fighting over the governance of Dublin, which allowed Irish monarchs to end the rule of Viking descendants at the close in the 10th century.

At the time of 980, Vikings were considered subordinate and required to give tribute to the Irish however, they continued to live in the cities they been settling in, and they still controlled trade across the globe, which the Irish appeared to have none of interest in carrying out. About a hundred years after that, both cultures had merged almost completely and are evident through cultural artifacts, coins, as well as in the documents written. Irish Kings inhabited old Viking cities and Vikings were involved and battled alongside the Irish with respect to different sides of their battles. Many prominent people of their time are mentioned within both Icelandic epics as well as the Irish historical accounts, but there are some differences between them.

The thing that would ultimately hinder this peaceful coexistence was English invasion of 1170 in which Dublin was taken over by English control, removing the Scandinavian cultural and culture and. There are remnants of Norse are found in Irish specifically, in particular words that relate to the sea and sailing. Ireland has a wealth of writing sources from the past The monks and scribes of the monasteries kept documents, and they wrote down the Annals of Ulster are an significant source of information about as well as the Vikings as well as Irish activity within the island. Scotland does not have any original documents written in the past and a large amount of information can be gleaned from archeological excavations, locations of names, as well as more recent chronicles as well as epic sagas.

A greater quantity of hoards of valuable metals have been discovered in Ireland as compared to Scotland This is a sign of that the wealth coming to Ireland as a result of it's Viking trade. The metals of silver and gold were discovered throughout the Viking Age, usually in the form of arm-rings jewelry, ingots, coins and other fragments similar to ones found for the Scandinavian economy simultaneously.

There are also records of the slave trade that was the typical Viking trade. Also, remains of ceramics, glass silk, weapons and other materials were discovered from the continent of Europe as well as the eastern. However, only a few Viking graves have been discovered in Ireland which suggests that they were influenced by to the Christian religion at a young age and were then buried in accordance with Christian burial practices.

In Scotland in Scotland, the Vikings' greatest contribution was breaking the current power structures. Rivalry among the ruling tribes of Scotland and the various kingdoms of Scotland was fuelled through the arrival of Scandinavians as well as the very short time, the Scots utilized the turbulent conditions to their advantage. They defeated other tribes in order to gain supremacy over the entire country.

England

England at the time of the Middle Ages consisted of five distinct kingdoms. The frequent Viking attacks did not to settle the feud between the King and his. All of the island was witness to the rise of cities with wealth however, unlike Ireland however, it wasn't exclusively monasteries that were hit during the robbing. England was set to be one of the main sources of revenue to the Vikings.

Alongside taking pillages and looting, Vikings additionally claimed vast territories in the form of Danegeld were traders and carried out many trading in the region. Following the initial phase of fighting, the Vikings settled down and cultivated their lands. They also built towns and were able to take on kingdoms they had already conquered and eventually laid the groundwork for a time that would be a period of Viking rule throughout England.

In the span of more than two decades England as well as Denmark would have the same king, and he made his mark on both English as well as Scandinavian cultural. This aspect of Viking time is documented however, the documents mostly written by people who were oppressed or the victims and thus heavily biased. Along with archaeological findings and evidence of linguistics There are a myriad of stories to be told about this period of the Viking Age in England.

Other than the three attacks prior to 800, at Portland Island, Lindisfarne and Donemouthan There isn't indication of Viking presence before 835. The raiding started to be a reality, not only the war in England but also throughout Ireland and across the continent. Following this, England would see about 200 years of a growing Scandinavian presence, in various ways. This period of expansion started with the onset of a war in Sheppey the island at the mouth of river Thames located just south of London. England was split into five separate kingdoms in the period of period: Northumbria in the north; Mercia in the inland central region, East Anglia to the east, Kent in the southeast and Wessex to the south-west. for a lengthy period, Mercia had been the topmost kingdom among the five. However, since 800, Wessex gained this position, and became the most powerful opponent to Vikings and their expansion. It was also where the Danish Vikings was most prominent and the Norwegians were more inclined to go into the north before heading towards Ireland.

The larger waves of raids began in 835 the cities of Southampton as well as London received attacks just after Sheppey. They followed similar pattern to the initial raids against Lindisfarne and Donemouthan rapid arrivals, quick looting and burning, crushing, killing, as well as capturing prisoners Then the Vikings went away as fast after arriving. They set sail to reach early in the summer season, picked a few of targets for plundering then returned back to their home in fall. They waited another 15 years until any evidence was found of the winter-wandering Vikings and then an island off to the east of Kent known as Thanet.

In the following years, Sheppey also held Viking habitats, and was a kind of launchpad for attack inland. In 865 in 865, the Viking settlement in Thanet reached peace with the inhabitants of Kent to exchange cash, which was the beginning of many settlements that were to be paid by the people of the area to Vikings throughout England. The raids lasted along the coastlines of Wessex, Kent and East Anglia for several years. Once these initial efforts were successful the process did not last time before a full-scale army was able to reach the coast in East Anglia.

Between 2,000 and 3,000 people set sail from the coast in 865. The intention was to first attack and later to construct shelter and winterize at the beach. The army was more than just warring soldiers however, it also included women, slaves, and housekeepers to help the troops during their long time on the shores. It was the first attempt to end the cycle of fast-paced raiding and rapid plundering, and since the very first day, it was clear that this wave of Viking predations were unique in its own way. This force was destined to take over the land that were inhabited by the English monarchs and overtake the islands. They accomplished this feat with coordinated tactics including surprise-tactics, the gathering of intelligence and new alliances formed with local leaders who were rebellious. By combining conflict, looting, threats, and exorbitant alliances, they instantly destabilized the regions they invaded.

After negotiating peace with the people of East Anglia, the army began to move northwards into Northumbria in Northumbria, where a civil war was raging. The Viking army capitalized on the chance to take on the chaos and sacked York city York by a quick attack in the year the year 866. Just one year after the first settlements, which were temporary, in Kent in 866, the Vikings claimed one of the biggest English towns and centers of economic activity. The huge heathen army according to the name in its sources, was to remain in England for a long time, threating to spread destruction everywhere they went. Once they had made peace with residents of Northumbria they sailed into Mercia with little fuss, and appear to have settled down for the winter months without fighting occurring.

It was often simple enough to travel in the areas with a huge variety of disreputed Vikings in order to collect the slaves and loot in exchange in exchange for peace. A number of towns, such as London and Torksey just to name just a handful, got visits from the Vikings with no violent fights being recorded in the historical sources. After only a few steps across the island following year, the troops began to conquer the entire region that was East Anglia, during which they executed King Edmund and then moved on to Wessex around 870. Then, in Wessex they were met with more opposition from king Ecbert and nine major fights took place in the following year in the Anglo-Saxon Chronicle, along with several minor battles. The end result was that nine

Danish Earls and one King were dead, but before the two sides came to an agreement and the king Alfred the Great took over the throne.

Peace in Wessex and authority in East Anglia, and the leadership of York The army carried on their triumphant journey through the island for nearly 10 years before the pattern ended. Following the decision to expel King of Mercia from Repton and putting an unofficial puppet of the Vikings as the king, the troops suddenly opted to break up. The majority of the Viking army chose to go toward Northumbria under the direction of Halfdan who was one of the most prominent characters throughout Viking the history of. Like in traditional Viking style, they erected up camp in the winter months and went on to pillage, steal and then conquer the land in during the springtime, following which Halfdan handed over the plots of land to his friends. It was the beginning of the numerous Viking settlements throughout England as they moved further to cultivate and sustain their families while sailing across the sea similar to what they had been returning home to embark on a journey of adventure years before.

The rest of the troops was accompanied by three Danish monarchs, Guthrum, Oscetel and Anwend to Cambridge which is where they made camp and rested for a year prior to moving into Wessex seeking to force King Alfred to make concessions. Alfred eventually negotiated peace with them once more and they departed to take on Mercia by distributing their lands to troops eager to settle following years of scurrying and fighting. The peace agreement with Alfred was broken up and it was later revised, allowing the kingship of Guthrum as the king from one of the three kingdoms that were in England which was then under Viking rule. After fifteen years of the presence of the huge heathen army in England it was able to conquer all of the country and brought it under Viking rule. However, it was a huge task that required a long time to accomplish.

Due to the negative image that they gained by shooting monks and attacking monasteries They did not need to fight nearly as hard as we are led to believe. They deliberately cultivated the image of fierceness in their actions and were able to respond to psychological warfare in lieu of engaging in a complete assault. A few of Viking behaviors, like showing dead bodies or degrading the deceased, served to inspire fear among possible victims, who agreed to make peace in advance to avoid a fight with those of such low morals. For peace, the Vikings were able to request whatever they desired including accommodation, treasure horse, supplies hostages, oaths or specific agreement. In the end, the Vikings started their quests in order to make money rather than for the killing and warring part of the expedition. If they managed to acquire wealth without the sacrifice of the horses, people or vessels it was obviously more desirable. Whatever the picture of them is depicted from the source materials there was no doubt that they were rational men. The harsh winters, the outbreaks, and a tough life style that was rooted in apathy had worn out the army of heathens in England And with the secure boundaries drawn out in the most recent agreement to end the war with Alfred the majority were of them decided that they were ready to settle. Only a few, or possibly none seemed to have an interest in going back to Scandinavia after a long time away.

In the wake of stable and peaceful conditions, certain members of the military fled to the city of Ghent within Belgium that witnessed increased Viking action, but the majority of the soldiers resided in one of several areas that were under their supervision. At the close of the 9th century, the times became difficult also across the continent since the earls and monarchs of Frankia enhanced their fortifications, and had the ability to better defend themselves against Vikings. The first Viking army was forced to flee Frankia and landed in England hoping to be settled as their benefactors were able to do, but this time, King Alfred refused to let the Vikings go. The King chased them around the land for three years, before they finally gave in and retreated towards the north to Viking Northumbria and East Anglia.

The next-of-kin of Alfred the Great ensured that they honored his legacy and to affirm Wessex's sovereignty while extending its influence to the north. Northumbria as well as York were under Viking rule through the larger portion of the 20th century, often snubbed by determined English monarchs of Wessex. Wessex will not cease until York came subordinate to English rule again In 954, the final Viking ruler from York, Erik Bloodaxe, was exiled from York and executed in Stainmore located in Northumbria. This was the first instance in the history of mankind that England was united under one King, Eadred, and all remaining Vikings within England were now under the rule of Eadred. It is what happened when the Danegeld or Danelaw in the sense that it's known in the present day English came into existence although it was not recorded in any source up to the 11th century.

The Danelaw refers to the power of the Viking controlled areas in England. The Vikings were no longer the rulers of these lands until this moment, but they were able to make their own laws in the context of English rules. This allowed the Vikings preserve a bit of freedom, yet it hindered the kind of integration happening within Ireland. The development and widespread utilization of the Danelaw is among the main factors that influenced the establishments that took place in England. Once England was united, and peace brought peace, many towns were able to begin to develop and flourish. It is interesting to note that many cities and towns that were established in England at the time or soon after had been so due to Viking actions. The fortifications of King Alfred grew into towns. The wall enclaving he constructed around certain castles and churches eventually attracted a large number of people seeking shelter behind the gates that were large. The Vikings' villages also transformed into towns once the English were in power due to their position as well as the fact they already had centers of administration as well as urban structures. York and Lincoln are two of the biggest towns in the present were founded by the Scandinavians and became influential during their time of rule.

Additionally, there are a large variety of terms in the contemporary English languages that have Scandinavian sources, like typical everyday phrases and plenty of words about sea and ocean-related. When it was the case in older English dialects there was many words that were related to agriculture. However, they are now out of usage since different dialects disappear. Another example of Viking influence on English cultural landscape can be seen in the various name variations, which end by a variety of suffixes, such as such as -by, -

thorpe or the suffix -ton. Also, there are a variety of "scandinavisations" of some names that were previously English but are nowadays spelled with a traditional Scandinavian manner, or directly translated, such as Kirkby (which was once Churchton). There is also the option to make use of the names for places to determine where Danish or Norwegians resided.

As in Ireland like Ireland, Vikings were in England were also able to adopt Christianity quite swiftly. Following the initial attacks of monasteries and churches completed and the raging force of Vikings quickly stopped and decided to establish themselves in various parts of the island. It took only a few days before the first king of Vikings, Guthrum, was received a baptism. In 878, he embraced the new religion and named Athelstan. In the records of the second half of the century end talking about the Vikings from southeast England as a heathen, which suggests they had been converted by this time. The transition in the north was not as easy and it was a long time when the two views interacted. A few burial sites contain traces of Christian as well as Pagan traditions, and some coins that date from the early part in the 10th century have been made bearing the saint's name on one side, and Thor's hammer in the opposite. Additionally, gravestones and crosses of the period bear designs from Pagan mythology. This was frequently discovered in Ireland as well, even though they were Christian memorials.

The initial turmoil slowly ended throughout the British Isles, the more active Viking journeys took place both to and from Scandinavia. A stalemate in the relationship between King of England and Ireland as well as the Viking rulers resulted in the decline of Viking activity for nearly fifty years, we are told that the Scandinavian inhabitants enjoyed peace and tranquility under English administration. The situation changed in both Europe as well as in England in the year 982, when the king Edward of England passed away in mysterious circumstances and was succeeded by his comparatively young daughter, Aethelred. The result was a fresh increase in political instability and was immediately followed by new Viking attacks in the years 980, 981 and 982.

It was almost that they had retreated and arrived in small groups in order to study potential possibilities in the island. Following successful victories and victories, the Vikings returned in the following years with a huge fleet and many thousands of troops, under the direction of the future leader of the kingdom of

Norway, Olaf Tryggvason. This was the second time Viking battles that took place in England was documented within the Anglo-Saxon Chronicle on an almost every year basis. It provides a variety of explanations for why the Vikings were able to conquer all of the country in just a few years. The reasons for this included poor luck, recklessness, cowardice, and treachery decisions, as well as a younger ruler named Aethelred. In order to stop the devastation of the Danish army, the Danish army received huge tributes to gold and silver not less than three times over the next time, and it took several pleas from the public before Olaf and his comrade Svein Forkbeard opted to go to England for home.

The riches they taken home during these many years of raiding Olaf was able to easily return to Norway to claim the throne, armed with his acknowledged ability and riches. In the end, Olaf would lose a battle with his former friend Svein. The stories of the infinite riches of England were quickly spreading across Scandinavia and made it possible to assemble large groups of soldiers to take on raids repeatedly. Riding through England was a high-profile activity for everyone Scandinavian males, and throughout this period, more runestones were erected to commemorate people who crossed the ocean. The beginning of the 11th century witnessed several Danish armies arrive in England and with almost ease, they brought a wealth of wealth back to home. Svein Forkbeard was one these chieftains, who came again and again, and decided to end the truce with Aethelred. The chieftain returned with an enormous army to take over the southeast and south of England at the beginning in the eleventh century. Aethelred quickly responded with his own response, and in the year 1002 the

King made it a rule for the entire population of Danish people throughout England to be put on trial the 13th day of November of that year.

Although he might not have wanted the older Scandinavian groups to be hurt in this vengeance-driven act Many people perished their lives on that day. It triggered another cycle of raids in which additional Danish chieftains came in the year 1006 to continue for five more years of continuous fighting. The English monarch was frequently required to pay huge tributes to help save the country and its inhabitants from the Vikings who were furious. After 10 years of going and moving, broken promises, fighting and paying tributes, Svein began what was to be his last battle against England and his son Cnut. In the end, he was able to conquer Danelaw and then the western and southern regions and west, he was able to take over the entirety of England as his. Aethelred as well as his entire family moved to Normandy however, they were soon able to return back to the country they grew up in following Svein was killed in 1014.

It was the Danish army was driven back to its homeland, but it returned stronger and more determined in the years that followed, led by an older Cnut. Cnut prevailed during the subsequent battles and reached a deal along with Aethelred's successor Edmund who wanted to divide Denmark into two countries and control half of it at a time. It was not put into effect, as Edmund died just a few days after the deal was made.

Cnut was proclaimed to be the sole leader of England and proved to be extremely competent. He was able to bring peace and stability on the island and due to the close relationship between Denmark and

Norway that he was able to conquer and control to stop the possibility of further Viking attack against England. He threw out the nobles from his past and established an aristocratic new order, having a smaller fleet of forty ships, in order to keep people aware of his Viking history. Through other means, he transformed into a pious Englishman with a large amount of respect to the Christian government, creating churches, going to Rome as well as establishing friendships with German Henry the Emperor. Henry. The king was respected throughout his territory and, during his time as a monarch and king, England was able to be settled and stabilized.

Obviously, when he passed away in 1035, the situation was to be a chaotic time and the empire he built would was divided. Norway, Denmark, and England are now a part of one but the bonds that he established between them were to be the start of the ending of the Viking Age in England. Scandinavia was becoming Christianized and the society was rapidly shifting. In the time of his rule, many notable literary and artistic figures traveled between nations, bringing influences from all across the continents. There are numerous evidences of Scandinavia throughout England at the time and the reverse route around. The three nations merged into one space which meant that Scandinavia was open for international exchanges to greater extent than prior to. England had be patient until the year 1066 before another powerful ruler to take the power of his reign and restore stability to the nation. In 1066, William the Conqueror who was also believed to have Viking descendance, would come in to unite the country that had been divided. In his time it was a failed attempt by the Danish ruler to conquer England However, William was steadfast and protected his land.

Chapter 4: Mainland Europe

The Vikings made their first appearance on mainland Europe was recorded by the Frankish Annals of 810 when they first began to show up in Frisia in the time in between the wave of raids that occurred in England. The raid had a different style of attack compared to battles that took place in England This distinction would be applicable to Vikings actions throughout Frankia as well as around the continent of Europe. Denmark because of its proximity associated with Europe, can gather information on the political and religious developments of Frankia that spread quickly over the border into Scandinavia. This is likely the reason what caused the first incident in Frisia was a success [editor's note: ??] at first, it was driven more by political reasons more than the desire for adventure and the dazzling loot that been the driving force behind the raids on in the British Isles.

At the start 9th century in the 9th century, Danish King Godfred was planning to construct walls between to the North Sea to the Baltic with just one entrance accessible through Hedeby and Hedeby, which would make the capital of Hedeby an essential route for the goods going to the north. The wall was intended to function in order to keep Charlemagne as well as his brutal pursuit of evangelism to other cultures away from Scandinavia and also to show that the Danish were not going to yield to the demands of Charlemagne. Charlemagne was attempting to create an alliance with English rulers in order to take over Denmark as well as the remainder of Scandinavia however, he would be devastated by the very first of a string of Viking attacks before he had the chance to organize this mission. Since he was Charlemagne He, however did not get swept away and was astonished, yet he knew about King Godfred's thoughts that were originating from the other side of the line. The moment King Godfred was accompanied by nearly 200 ships, he began raiding Frisia Charlemagne went across the river to join the Danish army at the mouth of the Weser river. Weser. Godfred was murdered in battle by one of his soldiers and his successor was reconciled with Charlemagne and ended the war just before it began.

After Charlemagne passed away in 814, his fortifications were massive around the coasts, deterring Viking assaults for another decade, making it impossible for them to build energy through Frankia as well as Frisia. It could have been the beginning for the Viking explorations across mainland Europe if it weren't because of the weakness in central power that the death of Charlemagne left in his wake. The son of Charlemagne, Louis the

Pious, was unfortunate to be being the third of three sons with ambition who could not sit around waiting until he died to take over the throne however, they were very eager to assume the throne of their grandfather. In Denmark the kings of three kingdoms disagreed over their decisions and responsibilities however one, Harald Klak, was in a good position with the newly appointed Frankish the emperor, no matter how the situation was a bit unstable currently. After Harald was banished from his home, and was given land at the river Weser with the understanding that he convert to Christianity and defend Frankia against attacks from north.

It was the very first of the Scandinavians who settled along the shores from the Frankish empire. He fought his earlier allies. The same time, Louis the Pious was captured by his three sons, who had a difficult time deciding which way to run the Empire. Practically speaking, he continued to rule while his three sons were unable to gather enough support to allow a complete taking over of the power. The weakened situation and the nobility that began to seek new loyalty, made way to the possibility of Viking explorations that correlated precisely with the subsequent wave of raids in England. Dorestad, a major trade hub Dorestad situated on the Rhine, which is located on the Rhine in Germany, was attacked and pillaged four years over a period of time, from 834-837. There is a good chance that the attacks were commanded by Harald, the previous Frankish allies Harald as well as others insurgent Viking tribes benefited from the internal conflict.

Louis the Pious took up a lot of his time as a monarch making fortresses, defence outposts and fortresses until he passed away in the year 838, and the kingdom was divided between his three sons following his death. They struggled hard to stop the flow of growing raids, but the Vikings increased in efficient in their efforts, and learned to take on bigger cities using new strategies as well as better weaponry. In large part, they could, just like England avoided fighting with tributes that were demanded by many of the towns as well as local communities. Also, they were aware of occasions when Christians were taking part in mass or huge Christian celebrations would take place in order to strike when their victims are not prepared or in their most vulnerable. In Nantes 843, they anticipated the awaited St John's Day when the city would be brimming with events and large numbers of tourists, which would mean an increase in targets for plunder. The attack may have been initiated by the cooperation of a rebellious count who refused to follow the reigning King Charles who was one of the children of Louis. There are numerous documents that suggest that the three brothers enlisted the assistance of Vikings in a bid to battle and collaborate with each other. And all the Frankish King was left defenseless as the Vikings came to town.

It didn't take long years until an army comprised consisting of Norwegians, Danish and probably Swedish made it across the Seine to attack Paris and was able to steal their way into the very heart of the city: Ile of the Cite. The army had decided to use Easter day for the strike, which was an extremely favorable date for Christians however, even though they took more riches and loot from Paris than any attack during the time of Frankia prior to that, their returning of the troops was hampered due to an epidemic that killed of more Vikings than they could spare. The incident led to an apology by the Danish King Horik and he let go the entire group of Christian prisoners he'd taken in a raid on Hamburg earlier in order to placate the Gods with their rage. However, the successful raid on Paris was not enough to quell the Vikings desire to plunder, however horrible the result has been. In the 860's, records reveal an extensive listing of Frankish monasteries and towns that became prey to the Vikings who ravaged the area; Bordeaux, Perigueux, Angers, Limoges, Angouleme, Tours, Toulouse, Orleans, Rouen, Paris, Meaux, Melun, Chartres, Eveux and Bayeux. One way or other, these cities were targeted in the raids. Some were attacked and some were simply threatened with the threat of an attack in the event of not paying a tribute.

The Vikings focused on monasteries and cities during their raids. They did not go into the countryside as often as they did in England In the beginning of the 9th century, there was a variety of diverse armies on the beaches as well as the rivers of Frankia. Actually, there had so many armies that Frankish rulers, Lothar, Louis and Charles put them up against each other in order to drive them from their lands. It was an effective strategy as it was unsuccessful, and, in 864, the backing of Viking armies had to be ended in every manner. selling a horse or a weapon to an Viking was now punished by death. The Frankish army sought to fight the war by using burning. With better tactics building fortifications, and battling in a brutal manner, they can take the Vikings from the countryside to the coastal areas and they were welcomed by the Franks permitted them to remain.

In the late 1700s, some members of Scandinavian fleets travelled further south. Records from the three countries of Spain, Italy and North Africa provide evidence of Vikings who visited. They were in large part engaged in the internal affairs in the Frankish kingdoms, and a number of Viking chieftains possessed the lands, riches and power primarily within Frisia at the end of the second quarter during the 9th century. Although they were meant to guard the inland from new attacks but they didn't bother with this task particularly. In the end, Dorestad kept seeing new wave of plundering over another two decades and Paris was under attack for more than two years in a time. In the year that the King of West Frankia, Charles the Bald was killed in 877. The next five years were marked by five distinct ruling families and a huge rise in Viking attack. When the English explorations diminished and the soldiers there opted to establish and began cultivating the land but those who were uninterested in this decided to move towards the less shaky West Frankish coast lines where the old kin of theirs are gaining ground. Then they moved throughout Flanders and through the Rhine and along the Scheldde. Schelde. Cologne and Trier were destroyed, while monasteries in remote areas had to endure severe attack.

The whole thing ended abruptly after the emperor of the day, Charles the Fat was able to get the Danish King who was leading the attack executed. The lack of power in the Danish management created an opportunity for the emperor to hit the Danes to the point that they could be unable to return. Following a myriad of bargains, bribes, tributes and compromises and tributes, the most affluent of Viking explorations was coming to an end just like the 9th century was also. After more than eighty years of constant attacks with deceits and alterations to structure of power, the Franks have finally learned how to defend themselves against Scandinavian fleets. Gradually, they were able to defend themselves. Vikings were also able to stay in the territories that were given to them to protect themselves their homelands, however the majority migrated to England in the midst of England, where Vikings enjoyed vast kingdoms under Scandinavian control, and were able to live in areas where they lived with relative peace. When the third and fourth big waves of raids struck England following the death of Alfred's death. Alfred had passed away in the year 146, it was clear that the Frankish kingdoms were largely unaffected.

The 10th century was a time when Western European kingdoms stabilised and increased in strength, but the

Germans and Franks drove the Vikings across the river and threatened the borders to Denmark. There was a single established settlement called Normandy that was where Rollo held Rouen. Rollo was a ruler of Rouen however, other than that, the Vikings were unable to make any failed attempts at raiding Frisia and the surrounding area, but they proved to be quite disappointing in comparison to the riches found in England. Rollo and his family stayed for a long time in Normandy for a long time and were able to increase their reach over more territories that anyone else Viking leader in mainland Europe in the period. In the region that we can discover more archaeological treasures as well as place names, and other evidence of Viking activities from across Frankia as well as Frisia. In addition, there are only a few physical evidence of their infamous raids. However, we do have a good amount of reliable written sources that provide information on the exact nature of attacks, which were brutal targeted, direct and focused on the securing of slaves and loot. But, it's also well-known that Vikings were often more interested in war in a way to threaten their enemies than an actual desire to participate in. They were mostly focused on silver, gold as well as slaves, never fighting for fight's purpose.

The major difference between raids that occurred in England as well as those which occurred in Frankia did not lie in their intentions however their outcomes. Although both English and Frankish kingdoms were afflicted by internal conflict as well as political machinations however, the Vikings were unable to conquer the land in Frankia the way they did in England. The Vikings did not intend to cultivate the lands or move in, rather they raided towns and monasteries with violence to steal wealth and plunder for their return with a sense of glory. The influence of Scandinavian tradition in Frankia was much less than that of England And, aside from some remnants of their activity including just one Viking grave, an atypical sword and coins, there aren't much evidence of their existence. The same is true for the fact that there are only the usual names and names of places in Normandy which is where Viking descendants ruled throughout the many centuries. Numerous Scandinavians moved to the fertile soils to cultivate and settle in the area, and Rouen was a flourishing trade centre. The majority of these were Christians were baptized and had Christian names. This saw the traditional Scandinavian names disappear rather quickly in the source books, and their use as popular names did not extend beyond the borders of Normandy. Normandy, the name of the place itself

Normandy is probably one of the most prominent place names that was used at the time. It translates to "land of the Northmen".

There are a handful of others with similar names however, the majority were adopted into the Frank language following the retaking of Normandy in the year 1204. The effect that the European raids made on Scandinavia were greater and in some ways superior to the opposite because of the huge collection of silver and gold which ended onto Scandinavian soil, and contributing to the growth of cities as well as the kings. Large quantities of wealth would power the success of expeditions that headed towards England every time as well as those that aimed further to the east and south. The construction of large vessels with such a large number of ships as accounts of England at the end of the 11th century probably wouldn't have been feasible without the huge inflow of precious metals as well as stones from monasteries. The raids that occurred in Frankia and Frisia contributed more to Vikings returning the treasures to Scandinavia as it did to the kings, chieftains monks, and priests who were displaced by their possessions. Though the events were extremely frightening, traumatising and painful for the people who lived through them, their most notable results were observed in missions such as those which Svein Forkbeard Olaf Tryggvason and Cnut the Great led toward England.

Chapter 5: Further West

Around the end of the 860's Vikings who had hopped islands across in the North Atlantic came to Iceland that was completely established by 930. Although Iceland is now forever associated in the history of Vikings, Irish Christians had existed living in Iceland prior to them. Irish Christians had been in Iceland long before the arrival of the Vikings. They were sailing there in small circular boats with skins that were covered in a kind of leather named coracles. These voyages might have been to allow their Irish monks to live an isolated and contemplative life. According to legend, one of the Irish monk St. Brendan saw the enormous volcanic eruption of Katla which is currently under glacier Myrdalsjokull located on the southern coast.

However, the vast majority of the Viking families that settled in Iceland could have been aristocratic families from the past of Scandinavia who were dissatisfied with the plans by King Harald to increase the size of the boundaries of his Norwegian Kingdom. The Vikings surely were delighted to discover Iceland practically uninhabited, and this was especially since the island, which was surrounded by trees, was then enjoying an arid climate. In the Medieval Warm Period or Little Optimum between 800 and 1200, Iceland was virtually free of ice and made travel on its shores a secure. Massive tracts of land could be used for pastures and for the cultivation of grain.

The Viking inhabitants of Iceland didn't want to see their complaints taken to Norway to settle and so they adopted the concept of a local body or the Thing common to them under the Norwegian administration prior to the reign to the throne of Harald Finehair. Iceland was split into regions that were with the authority by a chieftain. his supporters were known as Thingmen. At first, there were 36 chieftains however, the number was increased by 39, and later 48. Legal issues were debated every spring during local gatherings of the Thing as well as a larger assembly, or Althing took place for two weeks during the last week of June in Thingvellir or on the Assemly Plain. The person who presided over the Althing was the Lawspeaker who was elected for a term of three years. The Lawspeaker quoted out of the Law Rock the legislation passed by the Althing's legislature known as the logretta. Concerning policy, he addressed and led participants of the Althing which included chieftains, who were obliged to participate.

Within the Icelandic Kristini Saga the history of the introduction of Christianity to Iceland is explained. As a possible companion to Olaf Tryggvason Thorvald traveled to Iceland and brought the beliefs of Olaf to the island. Christianizing Olaf to Iceland However, he did not succeed in convincing the Icelandic heathen leaders to Christianity as a new religion. Olaf later appointed Stefnir to promote Christianity to the masses, and did so with force, stomping around in the countryside, burning down heathen temples. In the end, Icelanders, who prided themselves as independent removed Stefnir and Olaf was then able to send Saxon "missionary" Thangbrand, who was also removed from the country and sent back to Trondheim.

In the story, Thangbrand had converted some Icelandic chieftains prior to his removal at the hands of these chieftains, who then were invited to visit Olaf on Trondheim. In the year 999, they set sail back to Iceland and went to the Althing this year in Thingvellir in which their influence was strong and it was determined by the Lawspeaker to establish only one law for Iceland and that it was to be the Christian one. There were provisions to allow for the disclosure of young children (mostly females) and the consumption of horseflesh as a ceremony, and the quiet observation of the right to perform ritual sacrifices in private were omitted in the law of the heathen. Even though an apocalyptic fight between the gods of the heathen and catastrophe of the earth were predicted by the gods

when they were threatened by a brand new God from the myths of ancient times but the emergence of Christianity in

Iceland was welcomed with an apprehension.

Illustrations of Erik the Red from Arngrimur Jonsson's Gronlandia.

The next installment in the Vikings Westward Journey revolves around the vibrant protagonist Erik The Red. Erik's father was criminally imprisoned in Norway because of murder, and then was exiled to Iceland and, as a result, Erik followed like his father's steps was at war with his neighbor. After Erik murdered his neighbor, the court ordered that he was exiled from an area of isolation in Iceland and then be removed from the country in three years. In the course of this exile in Iceland, Erik again fought with neighbors, and even killed one of them.

To avoid revenge, Erik fled away from Iceland towards a place that had previously been sighted by Icelandic sailors, who were exiled from their ship. Erik was sailing along the coastline of the land that he named Greenland. Although the term Greenland seems to be the exact opposite of what it actually is, in it's Medieval Warm Period Greenland was far from the gloomy like it is now.

Erik returned to Iceland and managed to market the lure to Greenland to 2 chieftains that accompanied around 25 ships full of settlers as well as their animals traveling to the farmland that was vacant in the west. The trip took four days. The number of the number of ships lost during the route or in journeys back to Iceland isn't known However, two settlements were constructed in the south part of Greenland and comprised of more than 190 farms and another farther to the west which had 90 farms. The first church built in Greenland was constructed in

Brattahlid (now K'agssiarssuk) by Erick's wife Thjodhild. The foundation outline of the chapel was exposed and a replica of the small church is being built near.

Reconstruction of Thjodhild's Chappel at Brattahlid, Greenland

The homes built by the colonists discovered in archeological excavations resembled ones found in other parts of the Viking diaspora, particularly in north. With a low roof and heated by a wood fire that was contained inside a ring located in the center, the homes generally had many rooms. The largest contained the animals. Furniture was more scarce, however certain houses might have maybe benches or even stools along the exterior walls. However, it appears that the Vikings from Greenland were generally squatting rather than sitting and squatting, as evident by pants that did not have a midseam on the seat, which have been found into European archaeological excavations. Females may have an individual room in where they could spin and weave. Tools for domestic use were made using soapstone horn and reindeer antler as well as wood.

In the years as the Medieval Warm Period came to its end, the life of the 14th century was becoming more difficult to Greenland farmers. In the winter, ice made access to beaches difficult and Thule-culture Eskimos came down from northern regions on the west coast before settling to the east of the coast. The Skrellings or, according to they were known by the Norse were known, fought the Viking settlements.

A century prior to the time that Eskimos were at war with Vikings There were instances when Vikings were traveling further to the west. To hunt seals, walrus, fish and other game species, Vikings traveled across over the Davis Strait in the 10th century and got to Baffin Island, as confirmed through archaeological evidence found at the site of Kimmikut. The westward journeys of the Greenlanders also involved long journeys towards the south along the coastline of Labrador. Evidence for Viking existence throughout North America comes initially from two epics: the Saga of the Greenlanders and the Saga of Erik the Red which is also known as the Vinland Sagas. The sagas, which were both recorded around 200 years later than the events that they recount are composed of oral stories that told tales of voyages to a different region by a variety of expeditions. They are all merged within the Saga of Erik the Red and the Saga of Erik the Red, in which it is stated it was Leif Ericson, the son of Erik the Red, led each of the expeditions, and was also the first to discover Vinland however it's more likely in an expedition led Thorfinn Karlsefni that Vinland was found. Three regions were identified by explorers who explored the American coast of the North Atlantic: Helluland "land of rocky slabs", which was identified by the name of Baffin Island; Markland, the coastline that runs from Ungava Bay south to the Strait of Belle Isle; and Vinland also known as "place where grapes grow".

It wasn't until 1960 that the exact location of an Viking settlement located in Vinland was located. The edge of the Great Northern Peninsula in Newfoundland, Canada, a small Viking settlement known as L'Anse aux Meadows was excavated along with the remains of three residence halls having been discovered. The halls were home to around 70 to 90 persons. Along with the halls that were covered in sod and a smithy in which nails were made as well as the small building for boat repairs were discovered. The theory is that this town could have been home to up to 500 people was one of two settlements named Straumfjord as well as Hop that are mentioned within the Saga of Erik the Red as the two Vinland base. L'Anse aux Meadows is thought to be one of the first as well as it is thought to be the latter. Hop was a summer retreat possibly as far in New Brunswick.

Native inhabitants in New Brunswick in the New World were referred to as Skrellings in the eyes of Vikings There are evidences that show they fought in a battle against Beothuks from L'Anse aux Meadows and the Mi'kmaqs further to the south.

Chapter 6: Who were the Vikings?

The Vikings were the people who lived in Scandinavian regions. The Scandinavian regions encompass countries such as Sweden, Denmark, and Norway. Naturally, Scandinavia was not always known as that. The word Scandinavia initially referred to the old Danish area of Scania and is now an Swedish region.

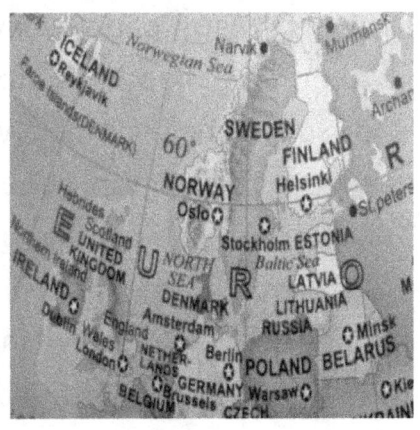

Map of Northern Europe

The Vikings moved out of the Scandinavian regions, and took on several areas of

Europe. They conquered the Frankish Empire (known today as France) as well as France, the British Isles, Iceland, portions of Greenland, Italy, and numerous other parts of Europe.

The Vikings weren't always referred to as Vikings. They were sometimes referred to as North Men, and some would call them Danes. Some people refer to them as "Rus meaning rowers. Many people have even described them as heathens for their vicious and sometimes violent ways of living. They were the English people were the first to refer to these people Vikings. A language that was once spoken by the ancient people of Old Norse, Viking is not a word; it is a verb meaning "to raid."

It is unclear the precise motive behind why the Vikings began leaving their Scandinavian homeland to attack other tribes to besiege them, but the main reason could be the fact that their homeland was getting smaller than they could handle and they needed to go. The Vikings increased their population rapidly that the landscape did not produce enough food to sustain the population. They wanted to become prosperous, which is why they went off to search for better landscapes. Because they were unable to build their own wealth so they opted to borrow the money from other people with pressure.

The Viking Age is the period that witnessed the frenzied expansion of the Scandinavian inhabitants across Europe as well as Russia. It started in CE 793, with the Lindisfarne Raid, when the Vikings quit Scandinavia and started to invade Europe.

The Vikings took their longships on board and set sail across the oceans to attack villages on the northern coast of Europe. The first place they came into contact was with the British Isles. The Vikings initially attacked England around 787 CE. They pilloried villages and racked up towns. The Vikings targeted monasteries that were not protected in their raids and gained the reputation of being viewed as barbarians. The Vikings were, however, not view it in the same as they did. They believed that monasteries as well as villages were rich and unprotected which made them easily targets. Anyone who was unprotected could be an ideal potential target. Vikings struck at places across the coastlines that comprised Scotland, England, Ireland, France, Italy, and even inland Russia. They pillaged, terrorized and traded, explored before finally settling and farming across the land they came across. Following their departure from the British Isles, they settled in what today is known as Northern France. After a short time in the area, the Vikings from Northern France broke away from the Vikings from Britain and began calling themselves Normans.

The Normans created a new Normandy country. Normandy that translates to "men of the north" and is an expression of the kind of people that Vikings were. North people.

The Viking Age

The Viking Age is a period that began 796 CE that lasted through 1066 CE. The Viking period began when the Scandinavian Norsemen departed their home in the in the upper nordic regions and travelled across Europe via its seas and rivers in search of trading, raids, the colonization of territories, and even conquest. In the Viking Age, the Vikings were settled on Norse Greenland, Newfoundland, as well as the present Faroe Islands, Iceland, Norway, Sweden, Normandy, Estonia, Scotland, England, Wales, Ireland, Isle of Man, the Netherlands, Germany, Ukraine, Russia, Turkey, and Italy.

The Viking Age began when in 793 when Vikings took over the abbey of Lindisfarne. It was a complex of structures where monks, nuns and other religious individuals came to study, live and perform their duties. It was in the past that the abbey was run by an abbot, or abbess. Lindisfarne was within Northumberland in the east coast of England. The Vikings murdered the monks, and dumped them in the ocean. They snatched away the remaining monks, and made them slaves. They also stole the abbey's treasures and stole each and every piece of wealth and cash. Following this event, the Lindisfarne residents began to say the prayer "Free us from the fury of the North men, Lord." The incidents of the Lindisfarne raid also led to the expression "wolves among sheep."

The Viking attacks destroyed the kingdom of the Franks in a significant way. The

Franks were a people living today in France. The Vikings were able to navigate to the River Seine easily and launch fierce attacks. This caused a pity on the king Charlemagne during that moment. Near the close of his reign, Vikings made further attacks at the Franks. After the Vikings totally defeated the Franks in the battle, they created the region later known as Normandy.

Following the establishment of Normandy and the Normandy region, several of the Vikings utilized their custom-built vessels, known as longships, in order to expand the reach that was the hallmark of Vikings. They cruised through Europe expanding the reach of Viking traders, pirates, and colonists further to the northwest of Europe. At this point there was a man called Rurik was who was a Viking chieftain, took control over a group Viking explorationists, and travelled eastward.

Slavic representatives before Rurik

The year was 859 and Rurik was a conqueror of several cities in the vicinity of River Volkhov. In the event of his death later, his heirs were called the Rurik dynasty, and carried on the legacy of his father by expanding Viking borders. They established their own kingdom, the Kievan

Rus' whose capital was located in Kyiv. It was Kievan Rus' became such a thriving city that it was the source of the foundations of the nations that are now Belarus, Russia, and Ukraine. In fact, the

Kievan Rus' was so significant that the capital city, Kyiv, never changed its name, and it is the capital city of Ukraine to this day. In the 11th century, it was the Kievan Rus' was so large that it extended all the way from to the White Sea to the Black Sea as well as from the start of River Vistula, which is the longest of all rivers in Poland as well as the 9th longest in Europe up until the Taman peninsula to the East. Due to the size that the Kievan Rus', it united several Slavic tribes from the east. The Slavic tribes lived in Central, Eastern and Southeastern Europe within the region known as Eurasia.

Its name refers to the Kievan Rus'. Kievan Rus' lasted until the 1240s, when the Mongolian tribes invaded and ruled Russia. In the course of the war, the Mongols took over several cities like Kolomna, Moscow, Vladimir, Ryazan, and many other. The Mongols also destroyed

Kyiv, the capital city. Kyiv. The Mongols took on Kievan Rus' Kievan Rus' in the Battle of the Kalka River in 1223 and throughout the many fights which followed. The victories also broke apart Kievan Rus' Kievan Rus' and divided the Slavic people into three distinct nations, now referred to by the names of Russia, Ukraine, and Belarus.

As these happenings continued throughout the East and to the West the there were other Vikings expanded over into the South Sea and even into Constantinople. Constantinople was the capital for Constantinople, which was part of the Eastern Roman Empire also known as the Byzantine Empire.

The End of the Viking Age

In 884 CE the Archbishop of Holland, named Rimbert of Bremen-Hamburg commanded the Frisian (Dutch) force in engage in battle against the Vikings from Denmark (also known as Danish Vikings). The battle occurred in Hilgenried Bay on the North Sea. The Frisian army was defeated by their foes the Danish Vikings and stopped the Norsemen from invading East Frisia.

The year was 911 C.E., in the year 911 CE, French Emperor Charles the Simple agreed with an Viking warrior called Rollo, who was the chief of Vikings who came from Norway in addition to Denmark. The agreement was that he'd grant Rollo the title of Duke as well as grant his acolytes the power over Normandy. The condition was that Rollo pledged loyalty to him and help defend the French from the other Vikings. Rollo accepted and was named his Duke Normandy. The people began calling him Rollo from Normandy. His family ruled over Normandy throughout the years when they attacked England in the Norman Conquest in 1066.

Rollo was also known by various names, as he was well-known among the Norsemen and French. His nicknames include Gongu-Hrolfr, and the Danish counterpart Ganger-Hrolf. Both names mean Hrolfr The Walker. He was referred to as The Walker due to the fact that he was so powerful and massive that people were shaken as they saw the man. In addition, he was so massive that a horse couldn't bear his weight and so his only option was to move on foot. After Rollo of Normandy was killed in 928 CE His younger son William Longsword, succeeded as his successor and took over Normandy. Duchy of Normandy that his father had constructed following the peace treaty signed in 928 CE with the King Charles the Simple. The Vikings from Normandy then identified themselves as Normans. A few years later, after the Normans defeated England they created the House of Normandy as a royal family. House of Normandy.

Rollo of Normandy is an important historical figure because he is the great-great-great-grandfather of William the Conqueror, also called William I of England. Due to his kinship with William I, he was an ancestor of the present British royal family and, by in turn, a ancestor to every currently European monarchs, as well as several contenders to the other European the thrones that have been long since abolished.

Rollo of Normandy's lineage lasted up to the year 1204, at which point the duke who was last in Normandy of the Rollo line, John Lackland lost his reign to the King Phillip II of France. The Rollo the dynasty endured the length of time it did thanks to a mixture of bloody military battles as well as internal conflict among individuals of the Frankish Aristocracy (the ruling families in France during the time) and resulted in them being severely weak and ineffective against those Norman Vikings' growing determination to keep their the throne.

The Viking period ended at the time when Christianity was very well-known throughout the Scandinavian nations. Christianity quickly became the predominant religion of Scandinavia in the early 11th century. In 1030, there took place an epic battle dubbed The Battle of Stiklestad. Prior to that, Norway had never really been a nation in the true sense of it. There were kings from the local area throughout Norway that ruled their fiefdoms. Fiefdoms were tiny kingdoms, governed by a fief. A fief was usually a local ruler. In the late 9th century, an individual known as Harald Fairhair joined forces to Sigurd Ladejarl of Nidaros. The alliance ensured that the two men as well as their two fiefdoms grew strong and eventually they were able to control various fiefdoms. It didn't take too time for the entire fiefdoms to become the one nation of Norway and with Norwegians as citizens. The Norwegians quickly recognized Harald Fairhair as the first the king of Norway.

The alliance was not able to last time. Shortly after Harald passed away his ruling class (called the earls) of the city Lade and a few descendants of Harald struggled for control. The religion was a part of this lengthy struggle as it was politics, the two Harald's heirs, Haakon the Good and Olaf Tryggvason, tried to make Norway into Christianity. The year was 1,000 CE, Svein Haakonsson and Erik of Lade were the first to take over the control of the country. They were supported by the whole of their namesake, Svein's father and his father, King Svein of Denmark and the King Svein Forkbeard. In the year 1016, Olaf Haraldsson, who was a representative of the Harald's descendants Fairhair and Harald Fairhair, returned from one his Viking adventures to win election as King of Norway. In the following decade, in the year 1016 C.E, Olaf Haraldsson went to combat with the Earls of Lade in Nesjar and beat them.

An important event led to the victory of Olaf Haraldsson. The Danish King who had intervened in the Norwegian battle for power by backing the Earls of Lade had their hands full with their battles with England and were unable to hinder Olaf Haraldsson's ascendance to the top of the ladder. His victory, however, didn't last too long. The year 1028 CE was the time when The Danish king and king Cnut the Magnificent, signed alliances with the Earls of Lade and dispatched Olaf Haraldsson to faraway Kievan Rus' in the east. Then, a year later most recent Earl of Lade who was named Hako Jarl, was killed by drowning. As news spread to Olaf and he immediately returned to Norway along with his large troops to take over the crown.

Olaf was a soldier in an army of 3,600 troops across Sweden as well as the valleys of Verdal. A force of 3,600 soldiers in the time of Olaf was massive force. They occupied numerous valleys and mountains. They traveled 80 km to the north of the city Trondheim before arriving at Sticklestad. Sticklestad was a small farm situated in the lower region of the Verdal valley. Olaf and his troops fought with the Lade Army of 14400 soldiers which was led by three men, Harek of Tjotta Thorir Hund from Bjarkoy as well as Kalfr Arnason. The two armies battled in Sticklestad during a bloody fight. Olaf's forces fought into battle shouting, "Forward, forward men of the cross, men of the king!" and the Lade army predominantly of peasants, cried "Forward Forward! Farmers!" Olaf Haraldsson died during the battle. Thorir Hund delivered the fatal strike in the battle after Olaf was severely wounded. The men took his body and laid it to rest on the shores of the Nidelva River which lies at the southernmost point of Trondheim.

A year later, after the war After the battle, Norwegians went to the tomb and found Olaf's body hadn't been decomposing. His hair and nails were even growing following his death. The authorities were not able to comprehend this marvel, therefore they took his body to St. Clement's Church in Trondheim.

After Olaf passed away his family, nobles and wealthy farmers who believed that

Olaf's demise was going to end competition and help them gain prominence soon realized they were mistaken. Instead of gaining influence, they were relegated by the mistress of King Cnut who was in charge after her lover passed away. Remember that the King Cnut was the Danish ruler who sent Olaf out of the country. The son of his mistress, Svein, was a extremely harsh ruler who put them through hardships; He did not save the church. The church was most affected due to the fact that it had been a supporter of Olaf. In this way, Olaf's passing became increasingly significant. People of the commons and a number of nobles of lower rank considered Olaf to be a martyr, and even supported him even though he'd never been an ideal leader. A martyr is one who dies due to their religion or any other belief. They soon resisted the Danish ruling class.

The events indicate that while Olaf Haraldsson was a stubborn aggressive, reckless and sometimes aggressive ruler when his reign was in place his fellow Vikings from Norway considered him heros in the end. Olaf Haraldsson was canonized one year following his death through the Bishop of Nidaros. What exactly does it mean for being canonized? Canonization is the process that declares someone, generally an unborn person, as to be a saint. In the wake of Olaf's canonization group of people gathered to form a cult, which brought the nation together and completed their goal of changing the nation to Christianity as the king of their time was fighting so long, and had even given up his life, to.

Chapter 7: Norse Mythology

The term "mythology" refers to a traditional tale that relates to the history of a group or explaining an event that is natural or social that is usually based on supernatural entities or events. A mythology is the collection of stories, with particular emphasis on those that is

associated with a specific religious or traditional culture.

Norse mythology, sometimes referred to as Scandinavian mythology, is comprised of myths and legends that were created by the Scandinavian people in the Viking Age. Norse mythology is more complicated than other mythologies. The mythology is rounded out with the creation myth, which involves the gods of the beginning slaying the giant before turning his body parts into world. According to mythology that the universe arose out of diverse realms, spread out under the World Tree named Yggdrasil.

Yggdrasil

The prophecy of the world's end was to be over in Ragnarok which was a sequence of events that included an epic battle which would cause the demise of the temple of gods.

Norse Cosmology

Cosmology is the study of the beginning and development in the Universe.

Cosmology is the study of how our universe came into existence. Vikings believed that the earth was be flat and was located in Yggdrasil. Yggdrasil was the tree of worlds which connected the nine worlds of Norse mythology. The nine worlds were: Niflheim, Asgard, Midgard, Vanaheim, Alfheim, Nidavellir, Svartalfheim, Jotunheim as well as Muspelheim. Asgard as well as Vanaheim were the homes of gods, and were located within the middle of the disc's flat area. Giants reside in Jotunheim and elves reside in Alfheim and dwarves are within Svartalfheim. Ice giants lived in the primitive realm of ice. Meanwhile, fire giants live in the world of Muspelheim. Helheim was an area beneath the Yggdrasil and was where the human race would stay after they die if the death wasn't honorable. Helheim was administered by an ancient goddess of similar name Hel. Dead souls were able to reach Hel (the the city) through the Gjoll river. Gjoll. A bridge crossed the river and was guarded by a female giant called Modgrudr. A sly dog called Garm along with its mate the rooster guarded the entryway to Hel's castle. There was no way to enter the castle besides dead persons. Once they had entered the castle, they were not able to quit for ever. The goal of Hel as a god of gods was to gather them in preparation in preparation for Ragnarok and the fight to end the world. The purpose of the rooster was to awaken souls of the dead.

Midgard was the place where people resided. It was located in the middle of an enormous ocean that was home to the huge sea serpent Jormungandr who swam through the globe. Midgard lies between Asgard which is the realm of the gods and Helheim (Hel) which is the graveyard that was inhabited by the deceased. It was the

Bifrost Bridge is the bridge that linked Midgard with Asgard. The god of Midgard, Heimdall, always guarded the Bifrost Bridge.

The Norse Mythology Creation Story

Prior to the time when the world according to how the Vikings believed began to form it was a two-world system. They were two distinct and different realms, one of which was the ice and fire. The realm of fire was known as Muspelheim and the icy one was known as Niflheim. In the beginning, Ginnungagap, an empty void, was the only thing that separated between the two realms. But afterward both the fiery realm and the icy one grew and joined. Following their battle and a stalemate, the cold realm of Niflheim was melted by the scorching heat of the fiery world, Muspelheim. In the midst of melting the ice, two bodies dripping out from the waters, the huge

Ymir and the cow Audhumla. Audhumla took a bite of the ice and revealed Buri who would become the father of gods. The son of Buri, Borr was able to join forces with Bestla and together they created the gods that were the first: Odin, Vili, and Ve. Three gods turned their backs on the gigantic Ymir to kill him as his size was enormous. In the event of their killing Ymir and buried him, they made use of the bones of his body to build the universe. The earth was created from his body and the sky with his skull, the ocean out of his blood, and the mountains using his bones. They created humans for the first time, Ask and Embala, out of two trees. Ask Embla and Embla were the first two couples.

The Supernatural Beings

The story of Norse mythology there existed gods, and other supernatural types that lived and existed in different ways.

Gods came from two families: one larger family known as the AEsir (pronounced "ice-y")) as well as the tinier family known as the Vanir. The AEsir included gods, who mostly participated in battle and ruled. The AEsir is usually used to refer to the most powerful and most strong gods. Odin, Thor, Baldr, Hodr, Heimdall, Tyr and Loki were all part of the AEsir family. The lesser Vanir family was home to lesser-known gods such as Njord, Freyr, and Freyja. The three gods of the Vanir family were fertility gods.

While all the gods resided in Asgard but they weren't all on the same page. The gods even fought numerous times. The AEsir battled Vanir Vanir while the Vanir were able to fight to defend themselves. The Vanir, on the other hand, generally immediately exchanged hostages and returned to peace once they had a period of time. The two had a mysterious relationship, as despite the fact that they tended to dislike one another, they did continue to marry.

The AEsir and Vanir Vanir varied in many ways, but most notable was their respective roles. The Vanir family was focused on the fertility of their harvests, abundant crops as well as the weather, and was a popular choice in agricultural societies of humans. On the other hand, the AEsir generally advised kings. Lords steered their warriors through issues of war as well as assisted the rulers of their respective families in the administration. So, whenever they AEsir as well as Vanir went to war, they had to work together. Vanir were at battle, they ultimately were forced to come to peace between each other because they realized they weren't in any way superior in any way than each other but they had to be able to support each other. Their conflicts and agreements are a reflection of the notion that a the society's functioning could only be achieved through the collective power of both classes.

In addition to from the AEsir along with the Vanir there were other types of divine beings, particularly female gods, were also present. The Disir were revered in private, while the Alfar or elves were supernatural entities with immense strength and were held with respect. Apart from these divine beings, there were the Jotnar giants as well as the Dvergar who were dwarfs.

Notable Supernatural Beings

1. Odin is also known as the Allfather who was the only-eyed hunter of wisdom. He is the God of war, magic and runes. He was hung on Yggdrasil for 9 days and 9 nights of gaining wisdom. The man who gave the runes humanity.

2. Thor The god of thunder, who held the magical war hammer Mjolnir was the protector of humanity as well as his kingdom of Midgard. He was a god of war.

3. Loki was the demigod who had a tangled web of demons. He was a half-blue gigantic. He was famous for his sleight of hand and deceit and usually was in charge of creating havoc with the gods.

4. Baldur was the son of Odin and Frigg. Baldur was gorgeous and generous god that everybody loved. However, Baldur was murdered due to Loki's tricks.

5. Frigg was the spouse of Odin. She was a magician, the goddess of the house as well as the mom of Baldur.

6. Freyja was the goddess with a feathered cloak of fertility and love. She also served different duties, including the death and war.

7. Freyr was Freyja's younger brother. Freyr was the god of agriculture, farming as well as fertility and wealth.

8. Njordr was the god of power of the sea.

9. Heimdall (also known as Heimdallr) was the god that guarded the Bifrost Bridge. He was the father of nine mothers, and various gods and even men who refer to him as "the" White God. Along with being the guardian of Bifrost Bridge, he also guarded Bifrost Bridge, he also protected the gods. He used to blow his Gjallarhorn horn to warn gods when Asgard were attacked. He was the strongest abilities in the universe. you could see even the end of the universe. He was able to hear falling leaves on the other side to the world. Additionally, Heimdallr never slept because the need to stay alert constantly.

Other Supernatural Creatures

The giants were a part of gods, however they were also their adversaries. They had always wanted to conquer the entire world. They would often attack humans and Thor was always on the lookout for him, equipped by his hammer of war, the magic Mjolnir.

The Dwarves were underground. They were blacksmiths and miners. Dwarves weren't short individuals like the majority of us believe; they were invisibly. They were powerful beings. They were gods of the night who could get married, have a mate with human beings and also give birth to kids. Two ravens, Hugin and Munin were kept abreast about everything happening in the world of human beings. Ratatosk was one of the squirrels who was a resident of the branches the tree of world, Yggdrasil.

* According to Norse mythology, the land spirits existed too. They were extremely

powerful and ruled those living in midgard. Midgard realm. Later on, under the early days of Icelandic legislation, Vikings had to remove dragon heads from their vessels when they approached the land to avoid offending the land spirits.

Chapter 8: Ragnarok

Ragnarok

Ragnarok refers to "fate of the gods" and is a reference to a sequence of events which were predicted as bringing about the demise of a variety of supernatural phenomena and even the whole world at large. In Ragnarok all gods were killed and the entire world was swept away into the sea. In the aftermath of Ragnarok it was over, the earth would come back to life and some gods returned to reign over the humans who were able to survive Ragnarok. This new group of human beings are the result of two mortals that escaped Ragnarok. Their human counterparts have names: Lif or Lifthrasir.

There was a belief that Vikings believed Ragnarok as a sign of the future. in the near future, however they didn't know the exact date the event would occur. The prophecy associated with Ragnarok was, however, a prophecy with immense implications on how Vikings were able to perceive the world of their times.

Based on the Ragnarok prophecy, female entities made and controlled destiny. These were the most powerful creatures in the Norse universe. They were even stronger than giants and gods, since they were also affected by destiny. The creatures known as Norns could one day decide the winter to be extremely cold, more frigid than anything the planet had previously experienced. Then storms would hurl violent snows in all directions. It would get so frigid that the sun would stop shining. The winter of the great one could be as long as three normal winters, and human living beings would starve to death of food. Mankind was starving to the point that they'd lose morality and humanity. When they were in this condition the people would care only for survival and begin to fight each other using weapons. The time of this would be known as the age of swords or Axes, where families murdering one another could be normal.

In the meantime there were two wolves called Skroll and Hati which had been chasing the sun and moon for many years, finally caught their quarry at last after which the stars vanished. In the wake of their disappearance there was nothing left and the skies would become black, which caused the Yggdrasil to shake. The mountains and trees were to fall to the earth as a result of the shaking. The chain that was keeping the beast in place, Fenrir snapped and the beast escaped. After Fenrir began to run free, Jormugand, the great serpent, which had been trapped to Yggrasil during all of this time, broke free and spewed the ocean over.

This tremor and the subsequent turmoil would shake the ship Naglfar (meaning "Nail Ship") away from its anchors. Naglfar was a ship made solely from fingernails and toenails of the deceased that was predicted to sail towards Vigridr carrying hordes who were to fight the gods. Vigridr was the vast area that was predicted to be the site of an epic battle between the armies of the gods and those of Surtr in Ragnarok. In Ragnarok, Naglfar would sail smoothly over the earth that was flooded and carry giants in their armies and those of the destruction. Loki was to be the leader of Naglfar who was officially declared to be unfaithful to Gods. Prior to this, Loki would have been locked up, but the chaos could have helped Loki escape. Fenrir was ablaze with fire out of his nostrils and eyes fled across the globe while keeping his lower jaw in the earth and his upper jaw pressed against the highest point of the sky and devouring everything that was within his reach. Jormungand unleashed his venom across the globe infecting the soil along with the water, air and.

The sky's dome was split, and fire giants appeared from Muspelheim. Surtr the leader of them and he held a fiery sword that was brighter than the sun in his hands. The fire giants made their way through to the Bifrost Bridge, which was the rainbow bridge leading to Asgard The bridge was set to collapse and disappear to the side of. Heimdallr, the godly sentry was the one who blew his magical warning horn Gjallarhorn which signaled the appearance of Ragnarok. Odin eagerly sought advice from Mimir's head Mimir to seek advice. Mimir was the most wise being on the planet, however the Vanir executed him during the war between Vanir and Aesir. The moment Odin was able to see the head that had been severed the next day, he carved it into a skeleton and applied special oils to it. He then sang songs of magic for it, then determined to keep the head. Therefore, whenever he required assistance, he would consult it and also the head of Mimir was able to advise him.

The gods were determined to face the fire giants of Muspelheim on the battlefield regardless of being conscious of the prophecy regarding the outcome of the battle. They prepared themselves for battle and faced the foes of their opponents on a battleground known as Vigridr.

The battle was a time when many gods took their own lives. Odin battled Fenrir and had the aid of an inherjar. The inherjar served as the home of his human warriors, whom he stored at Valhalla because of this. Valhalla was a place in which Odin held people who lost their lives, but whom he thought worthy of being a part of his. Odin as well as the Einherjar battled bravely however it wasn't enough. Fenrir beat Odin and his Einherjar. A furious Odin's children, a god of youth called Vidar and fought the monster with a ferocious attack by using a shoe for war that he designed specifically for the combat. The shoe was made out of all the fragments of leather human shoemakers had discarded over the years. This shoe Vidar kept

Fenrir's mouth wide open and cut his sword in the throat of Fenrir, killing him as well as avenging his father.

Afterward another wolf Garm as well as Tyr Tyr, god of justice and law fight each other, and then took their lives. Freyr and the huge Surtr murdered one another. Thor and Jormungand who were old adversaries were also fighting and killing the other. Thor did well in taking down the huge snake using the power of his hammer, Mjolnir, but Jormungand had covered him with such a thick layer of venom that he wasn't able to stay standing for very long and he had to take nine steps from his fight spot, before dying himself. Heimdall as well as Loki were the gods who left to fight, as well as killing their own gods, however Loki passed away earlier than Heimdall.

In the end, when all gods, giants and beasts passed away all the remnants of the earth sank into the ocean and the entire universe was an empty space. It was like everything was ever constructed had been reset like if the creation process and its existence gods, kings and humans were not even there at all.

For a considerable period of time the new world that was more lush and beautiful as the old one was born from the sea. The truth is that Vidar along with a handful of other gods like Vali, Baldur, Hodr, Modi, and Magni were able to survive the devastation of the previous world and were able to enjoy a life in the new. Two women and a man, Lif (meaning "life") and Lifthrasir (meaning "striving after life") and had been kept away from chaos and destruction within an area called"the Wood of Hoddmimir also came out to occupy the stunning new world. The new planet had the sun of the future, which was an offspring of the former one. The sun rose to the sky and shined brightly across the sky.

Chapter 9: What the Norse Mythology Meant to the Vikings

In Norse mythology In Norse mythology, the Vikings considered that the universe was going to end with Ragnarok. They believed that gods would be killed and the world would disappear into obscurity. Some believed that the universe would rise in the future, and that the earth could be born again with greater beauty and splendor. Indeed, a lot of researchers have debunked the idea of the mythology, which claims that a better, more beautiful world emerged. They claim that the introduction to that portion of the mythology to the mythology was added shortly after Christianity was introduced to Scandinavia. They claim that Christianity influences the Norse mythology, and then diluted the mythology. A storyteller and researcher, Daniel McCoy, wrote that the reference to rebirth was just from three different sources. The third was dependent upon the two other sources and all prior mentions of Ragnarok refer to the destruction and not ever mention any rebirth.

What was Ragnarok have to do with the Vikings in the past?

Imagine you lived in a universe in which everything seemed always in danger, regardless of how you acted. Also, the gods that you believed in and prayed to, only had limited power and were unable to stop the inevitable end. What would you do with your daily life?

According to many religious traditions of our time, once the world is over it is believed that there will be some kind of heavenly afterlife that which faithful and faithful individuals visit when they pass away. This isn't the case in the Norse Mythology at least, not in the old version.

If you were living in an environment in which all things would end up being destroyed and that the gods you worshipped were likely die with it but not any memory of any thing that existed was saved How would this affect your lifestyle? Do you think it would cast a shadow shade over your life? It's a complete senselessness, hopelessness and inanity will surely irritate you. It is possible that this was what the Vikings saw the world.

But, Ragnarok may also have given them other meanings. Although the idea that everything is in danger can be depressing, it might provide them with a realistic perspective of what they were living. Doom's prophecy didn't necessarily mean that they were despairing. The scenario of Ragnarok was also a source of inspiration for them. Since gods all were going to perish someday, human beings were going to die so it was just to say that gods and humans faced the identical fate. Furthermore, if gods could take on their demise in dignity, respect and courage, they could also do so for human beings. This is why the Vikings believed that fate and death should not simply depress or discourage humans and should rather inspire humanity to be exemplary and to perform acts of kindness - those worthy of leaving a lasting legacy for our descendants, long beyond our death.

Chapter 10: Viking Culture

Viking Man and woman

Many people think that the Vikings were merely plunderers and raiders. The media, as well as pop culture promote this notion. Films are watched and people think that the Vikings simply sailed across the globe in elaborate longships, then rowed between cities to burn buildings and plunder precious gold. It's not true This belief is exaggerated and focuses on just one aspect of Viking living.

Was it like to become an Viking during those times?

Occupations

Alongside being the plunderers, raiders and soldiers in addition, the Vikings were traders, hunter, farmers, explorers fishing, trappers as well as artisans. They were also fishermen, traders, trappers, hunters and farmers. Viking women were adept weaver and a textile maker. They created clothing using linen, wool, as well as animal skins. They transformed wool into yarn, and then dye the yarn, giving the colour. Once the Vikings got richer and robust, they started to create more elaborate designs for their clothing.

The Vikings were farmers. It was their main occupation since they required to cultivate enough food to feed their people and that's why they needed leave Scandinavia and seek out more lush grasslands to settle in. A typical Viking farm was tiny however enough to feed family members, enabling the farmers to become self-sufficient. The crops they cultivated included barley, grains as well as rye and the oats. They were able to make bread out of the grains, and create porridges with oatmeal. They were adept at digging dirt, they raised livestock, including chickens, cattle and goats, sheep, pork, and even breeding horses. They were skilled fishermen, and they hunted all types of aquatic creatures, from ordinary fish to whales.

Housing

The Vikings resided in basic, boxes-like homes. They built their houses in rectangular shapes, and often constructed from timber. In the event that they could not find enough wood, they'd use stone for dwellings. Contrary to popular belief, Vikings were very indoorsy individuals and performed the bulk of their activities in dwellings. The activities they did indoors were making clothes, cooking food and working with the leather.

Food

The Vikings ate mainly food from animals they kept. They ate meat from cattle, horses, goats and oxen. They also ate pigs, oxen and sheep as well as chickens and ducks. The cereals that the Vikings cultivated at their farms made up a significant part of their food habits. They made use of the oats and barley harvested for flour. Then they rolled it into dough before placing onto griddles for baking on open flames. What resulted from those baking sessions was Viking flatbread. The Vikings cultivated a wide variety of veggies such as onions, cabbage turnips, garlic, leeks as well as beans, peas and beans.

Weather

The weather played an important role in Viking lifestyle, and they needed to adjust their lives to the environment and the climate. If their hay or grass were not dry enough for winter, due to a rainy season or poor harvest they'd use fish as a source of protein, since they wouldn't be able to feed their animals. They analyzed the weather patterns forecasts, speculated about the weather, and determined the best time to sail. The Vikings are also known to pray and offer sacrifices for the god Njord for safe travel and offered prayers for Odin to have a favorable climate. Because of this, as well as keeping a close eye on the skies patterns, it was felt that they could have some control over the weather. If they had made a mistake and or made a wrong decision, they would lose their vessels in a severe storms. They were unable to travel in winter because of the ice that surrounded the seas and northern regions.

In spite of the extreme Scandinavian climate, the Vikings did not give up quickly. They even managed to create entertainment in such an environment. They came up with ways to deal with harsh winters through the development of competitive games such as snowball battles and ice skating. In this way they were able to improve their weather conditions and provide the form of fun ways to prepare children to fight when they grew older.

Language

The Vikings used a system of writing that had an alphabet with 16 letters. It did not contain any letters E, O, D, G, or P. This is fascinating and ironic in that the Vikings used these sounds in their language, but did not use these characters in their writings that depict the sound.

Although the majority of their language and tales were shared via words through mouths, there's only a handful of cases that show Viking writing. The Vikings did not practice writing, strictly speaking in the definition of "writing," rather, they made their message in runs on stones. The letters that run through the runes form a group of alphabets called runic alphabets that were employed to create in a variety of Germanic languages prior to the introduction of the Latin alphabet, and also for specific uses. A majority of runic stone keep stories of battles that were epic and also the stones that marked areas of territorial control.

Transportation

While they preferred to spend time inside, they also were extremely active and sedentary. They loved exploring the new frontiers and were great and skilled shipbuilders. The Vikings were the first to have a particular type of ship structure called longships (also known as longboats). They were extremely large and narrow. one of the reasons for this design was to allow them to navigate in shallow and deep water. They also assisted in raiding villages, by traveling up and down rivers.

The Vikings were the first to row their longboats as well as the standard rowboats. They made two types of smaller boats which included four and six paddles (or Oars) which men rode. Also, they built bigger boats that could have up to 50 oars, which could move the boat. When they were on land, the Vikings rode on horses or carts. In summer they would walk a lot and could make for long distances just by walking. The winter was when they travelled with sleds.

Religion

The Vikings were thought to be people of the paganism before they accepted Christianity. They're "pagan" religion was made predominantly of Norse mythology. At one point, they added a few elements of Christianity to their mythology when fighting Britain as well as France.

In the beginning, Viking Norse didn't take to Christianity. They worshipped their gods. However, even when the Danish or Swedish monarch was converted to Christian and declared that his subjects were required to change to Christianity However, many Norsemen kept their faith in their gods of the past. Converting Vikings to Christianity took centuries to complete, and by at the close period of the Viking Age, however, the vast majority of Vikings accepted Christianity and had been baptized into the religion.

It is not known what the Vikings were worshipping their Norse gods. However, like many pagan communities there were priests and priestesses. The historians have believed that Vikings might have offered sacrifices of horses in the name of gods. It is believed the Vikings believed in gods and the divine. They derived their beliefs from the Norse mythology as well as many other tales passed on through generations. Most of the stories the gods created the world from the sea and made Midgard which is where humans live. Odin The god of one eye of wisdom, war the justice system, death and poetry, is the god with the greatest power of Viking mythology. Thor is probably the most well-known god. Thor is also the god that is depicted in a variety of film and comics of superheroes from recent years. Thor was the god of thunder, and was armed with a powerful war hammer known as Mjolnir. The Vikings used the symbolism of Mjolnir frequently to be pendants and used these as symbolic totems.

Settlement

The Vikings were out of Scandinavia and settled throughout many areas. The first settled in British Isles and then they attacked Ireland, Scotland, and England. They also traveled to Wales as well as the Isle of Man. In the following years, Vikings traveled to France as well as sacked cities and villages in their Frankish Empire. In the course of time they signed an accord of peace in the Frankish Empire and subsequently settled in an area later known as Normandy.

As the Vikings made their home in Normandy but others Vikings scattered and began to travel to the south, until they arrived in Italy. Many Vikings operated as mercenaries throughout Sicily as well as Italy. There were Vikings were even further to the south and targeted the most northern regions of Africa. The Vikings expanded and spread until they covered the entire continent. An entire group of Vikings fled Norway, Sweden, and Denmark and went on long journeys towards Iceland, Greenland, and Canada. They arrived in Canada, Greenland and Iceland. Norwegian Vikings settled in Greenland before sailing their longships across Canada and sacked the country. Swedish Vikings migrated to the east, and eventually settled in specific areas of Russia. The Vikings were able to expand before they settled over the vast majority of northern Europe.

Chapter 11: Notable Viking Sagas and Kings

The Legend of Ragnar Lothbrok

Ragnar Lothbrok was Ragnar Lothbrok was a Greek King who reigned over Denmark and Sweden from the eighth century or the ninth century. The king was an outstanding hero however, nobody is certain of the precise dates of his reign or the time he lived. Many believe that he ruled from 750-794, while others believe he reigned in the 860-865. Many believe that his birthplace was in Norway before advancing to the elite of Denmark and became King.

His wife referred to him as "hairy breeches" because he liked trousers made of animal skin. In the course of his entire life particularly prior to becoming the king and the leader of a raider and pirate who sacked several nations. He also was an excellent commander in the military, however the man was overly enthusiastic and a lusty for his power.

Ragnar always declared, with pride that he was the direct descendant of Odin. He had a dislike for Christians and was known to attack Christian cities on the days they were celebrating their holy celebrations knowing that a lot of Christian soldiers were in the church.

Every time he fought and invaded the country, he would require huge sums of money to protect life of its people, only to go to the scene later, demanding more wealthy payments to let them go. He would always seek more victories, due to the fear that his children would accomplish things which would surpass his accomplishments.

On one day, he boarded 120 vessels with more than 5,000 Viking warriors, and set sail south looking for new territories to conquer. The Vikings landed in France near the Seine estuary and then retreated to West Francia which was the western region of the Frankish empire.

In March He defeated Paris and proclaimed the city. The significance of the battle remains significant across the globe. In Scandinavian nations today, people celebrate the 28th of March as Ragnar Lothbrok Day. The King of West Francia, a man known as Charlemagne, the child of Charles II "The Bald," offered him a massive sum of money and begged for him not to destroy Paris. Ragnar Lothbrok took home seven thousand pounds of silver return for the privilege of sparing Paris However, he continued into other areas of France. The Franks did not have the strength to stop at first, and it took would take a considerable amount of time (many several years) to thwart his efforts.

After capturing France after a long battle, he shifted his attention towards England. Around 865 CE when he set sail for Northumbria which is a region located along the coast of northeast England. At Northumbria, Ragnar Lothbrok tasted his first defeat during the battle. The King Aelle of Northumbria defeated his enemies and seized Ragnar. King Aelle instructed his soldiers to throw Ragnar Lothbrok in an area containing deadly snakes. He yelled "How the little pigs would grunt if they knew the situation of the old boar!" when he finally ended his ghost.

The moment Ragnar Lothbrok's children heard about the cause of his demise the entire family was saddened. One of his sons, Hvitserk had been playing chess when he heard the news. He gripped the pawn with such force that his fingers ran red. A different child, Bjorn, grabbed his spear with so much force that his palm nearly break it. His grip was tight enough that his palm made an impression on it. Sigurd the man who was slicing the nails of his mother, became amazed that he cut off his fingers so deeply that his bone was visible.

His fourth son the man who went by the name of Ivar the Boneless discovered the entire story and promised to be vengeful to his father's demise. A year later, in the year 866 CE, Ivar the Boneless traveled across his way across the North Sea with a large force and went to war with the troops of King Aelle. Ivar the Boneless was able to defeat King Aelle and then took his hostage. The King was sentenced by to the Northumbria King to be executed as per the customs of the blood-red Eagle. The custom of the blood-red eagle involved cutting the ribs off of the victim. They then removed their lungs, by gripping their ribs and spreading them throughout the body.

Ivor continued to make further savage attacks in the English mainland at the close of the 9th century. Ivor invaded East Anglia first, and followed by attacking York in the year following. The city was easily defeated by the cities due to already a struggle within the city to be the power of Northumbria making it hard for them to join together and defend their town. Naturally, the cause for the internal tussle over power began shortly after Ivar the Boneless defeated King Aelle.

As all of this was taking place in England and France it was the Vikings continued to return with more money to pay to secure the Franks liberation. The Vikings took over Rouen's city Rouen numerous times, however finally, they settled there forever, in the land known as Normandy.

Ivar the Boneless

Ragnar Lothbrok's son Ivar the Boneless Ivar the Boneless, was Ivar the Boneless, a Viking warlord, who was famous for his brutality. He was a fierce and violent person. He was known as Ivar Ragnarsson. People were known as Ivar the Boneless due to the fact that the fact that he didn't have any bones whatsoever and had only cartilage on the areas where the bones ought to be.

As normal human beings, we are blessed with both bones and cartilage The cartilage serves as a key structure of our body. It's a strong connective tissue that is found in a variety of regions of the body. This includes joint joints that connect bones e.g. knees, elbows and ankles. Ivar did not have cartilage in his knees, elbows, or ankles yet, strangely enough, Ivar was extremely strong as well as very tall, and extremely attractive. In battle it was his habit to tower above others, and always stood out. His arms were strong enough that his bow was larger and stronger than anyone else's. The arrows he shot were heavier than his fellow people.

Ivar the Boneless was a ruler of Denmark as well as Sweden. The reputation of Ivar the Boneless was being Berserker. In the past of Scandinavia Berserkers were Viking warriors that combative with an inexplicably violent rage and violence. This is the style of combat that the English term, "berserk," was derived from. Berserkers were known to have the custom to wear coats constructed from the bear's skin when fighting.

After his dad, Ragnar Lothbrok died by the hand by King Aelle who was a member of Northumbria, Ivar the Boneless traversed his way across the North Sea to England with his brothers Halfdan and Ubbe together with a massive force. They attacked East Anglia in the year 865 CE and pulled up the Viking Raven banner. Ragnar the daughters of Lodbrok (their sisters) were weaving their Viking Raven into the banner. The people of East Anglia quickly resigned and reached an agreement with the Vikings and providing them with presents as well as horses.

In the following one, Ivar took on York and captured the city. The city was then a target of a civil war in the nearby Northumbria. Aella was the most recent to take over the Northumbria throne from King Osberht who had reigned over the city for 18 years. In the event that Ivar The Boneless, his Viking army struck York but York was a place where Englishmen resolved their differences, and joined forces against their common foe. The Vikings 4 months to prepare for the battle. In 867 CE they sacked York's city walls, and attempted to conquer the city but they were unsuccessful. The Vikings killed everyone who been in the city, and killed all who were not inside. They took the two kings Aelle and King Osberht. Aelle as well as King Osberht and executed their kings as a retribution to Ragnar Lothbrok's brutal torture and execution. Ivar instructed his soldiers to put the King Aelle to the agonizing death of the blood eagle the gruesome and tradition Viking way for execution. The Vikings cut the King Aelle's ribs and spine they broke, then spread they in a manner they looked like blood-stained wings. They then Vikings took the lungs away through wounds in the back of his body. They sprayed salt on the wounds to ensure that the patient would scream in pain that was excruciating. They Northumbrian survivors fled north, then Ivar the Boneless crowned the name of Egbert as the puppet King of Northumbria.

Ivar the Boneless accompanied his Viking army into Mercia and set up camp in Nottingham. Befuddled, the king of Mercia, Burgred, sought the help of the Wessex king. The king of Wessex, King Ethelred (of Wessex) and his brother Alfred took action and accompanied their army to Mercia and attacked the Viking forces in Nottingham. Ivar the Boneless observed that Wessex and Mercia troops were far more numerous than the Vikings and he resisted to engage in battle. He spoke in a smooth manner and made diplomacy and made make peace with the Englishmen. He and his troops returned to York and became the most cruel of rulers.

Ivan the Boneless sent his army back in East Anglia when King Edmund of East Anglia led a resistance. King Edmund was captured and executed brutally in the town of Hoxne. The time of the Viking religious system of the time were a time when they disliked Christians and viewed them as followers of "White Christ.' They believed Christians were cowards and they would always be cruel towards their followers. Ivar the Boneless pleaded with Edmund courageously to abandon his Christianity and be his vassal. (A vassal is an official who is a landowner for the ruler of higher rank for whom he swore to be loyal.) Edmund was adamant, saying the importance of his faith was greater than his own life. So they beat him with clubs when his name was called out of Jesus. The Vikings were able to tie Edmund on a branch, and hit him with arrows until he passed away, and then they took his head off. The Vikings threw his body into the brambles deep in the forest and left the body to rot in the sand. After they executed them, they took down monasteries and massacred monks.

In the following years, Ivan the Boneless made friendship along with Olaf The White and was ruled by him within Dublin, Ireland. Ivan the Boneless and Olaf the White later launched a second assault against Scotland. They took over the Dumbarton Garrison for four months and cut off water supplies and also consuming the inhabitants living there by the thirst and hunger. Dumbarton Rock was awash with water. Dumbarton Rock defenders gave up after which the Vikings invaded to ruin the area. The Vikings came back to Dublin with treasures as well as slaves.

Dumbarton Garrison

Ivan the Boneless was killed in the year 873 due to a terrible, sudden illness that made him weak.

Erik the Red

Erik The Red Was Erik the Red was a Norwegian Viking who discovered and settled Greenland. The name he earned for himself was "Erik the Red" because the beard and hair that was in line with his flamboyant character were both the color red. The Viking often battled the people around him and was later exiled from Norway as well as Iceland. Once he had quit, he was one of the very first European settlement in Greenland.

Chapter 12: An Overview of Viking and Norse Mythology

Viking as well as Norse mythology is an investigation of the religion and culture of the Vikings as well as mythology that shaped the ethos of their culture. It's about figuring out what was going through the times and lives of the Vikings. It is also about analyzing what they did and why they were. A majority of their methods are considered to be myths in the present. It is a science that led them to being convinced of the foundational existence the manner they did, and how they interacted with creatures living within the firmament. Viking mythology refers to the compilation of stories, or folklore which became part of the persona they became. They are element of their heritage. This is the thing they came to be renowned for and the beliefs they held in. Through the narratives handed down from generation to Generations in the viking community and what is the religion and the culture of the Vikings could be found.

Folktales usually depict an element that transcends nature, and instill belief in the supernatural. The more stories like these were shared and listened to, the more people were influenced by them, and followed their advice to help inspire. The mythology of the vikings influenced their culture, tradition as well as their hierarchy, religion, as well as their relationship to the immortal, as they defined as it was. For instance, if one were to descend from the top of the hill, one might be looking to become an affluent member of the community, one is asked to be a part of the vikings. To practice their viking culture and submit to any authorities they consider to be ruling. It's not difficult to think that, since the vikings were warriors they could have had admirers in distant places that might have wished to come into their homes and become part of their people.

The new family who moved into the town was taken to the local chiefs and the kings to meet them and be welcomed. Then they were required to swear allegiance chiefs and vikings as well as the local population. It meant that they'd be part of the community as they practiced their faith and religious beliefs. When the village that was adopted would be involved in war, the family members were expected to take part during the war as well to participate in the prayer services that Vikings took part in before and after going to battle. The majority of movies today depict an intruder from a village, being taken to the chiefs' house and secured to the tree. The outcome is usually to end up in the hands of local soldiers. This ideal could have been drawn from the notion that the Vikings were the people of their territory and would not adore intruders as long as the invaders would pledge their allegiance to them, and their monarchs.

The presence of a newcomer into the village that did not have the same way of life as their predecessors can cause problems. The vikings firstly were interested in protecting their customs and practices, their religion along with the authority hierarchy as well as local resources. As the vikings were not have the modern technology us have at the time, they didn't have any other method to verify the intentions of a foreigner other than to remove it from the individual who had made the move. There was always a concern concerning the motives of the newcomers. Because the forefathers of the Vikings didn't have the same knowledge regarding science and technology in order for confirming facts, as the modern world and relied on folklore and superstitions. Folktales and superstitions could be the base on the basis for defining them or one another. The people whose beliefs about superstition were more similar to one others would join in villages. Vikings had similar beliefs and grouped around to share their beliefs and further develop their beliefs.

Human behaviors today could differ from the logic that was in place prior to Christ. While we've come to a point of knowledge and understanding, we are still faced with the same concerns within our heads that Vikings could have faced concerning their own lives. Who are we ? What brought us here What brought us now here? What happens in the afterlife? This is one of the most important questions that continue to occupy our minds even to this day. The vikings was the same. They attempted to address these questions through creating tales based on what they observed. They observed the seasons and the solar system the cardinal points, night and night geographic relief, animals in nature, births and deaths. In all the changes that occurred that were happening around them, they sought the explanation for why they took place and the reasons why they occurred in a specific way. They also wanted to understand how they humans reacted to the world things surrounding them.

In a bid to find answers to the most important questions of life They imagined the divine Gods, the firmament in the worlds of different universes, and the creatures that could live and exist in different universes. The soul-searching expeditions have led them to come to theories that would most likely reveal the fundamentals of existence for the people.

Their beliefs, rituals and beliefs gave rise to what's now referred to as Viking and Norse mythology. The collective practice of their culture gave them an identity and ultimately resulted in satisfaction. The feeling of satisfaction in the practice of their chosen culture and religion which kept them united. Every external threat, whether either real or imaginary, posed the threat of their newly established belief in their identity and the purpose of. This is why they'd want to conquer their foes and find the intruders and traitors.

Their faith-based practices led them to each other. They could find meaning any event they observed against the background of their religious beliefs. Each social event, whether either for celebration or tears, they handled the event in line with their religious beliefs and practices. When they were in good or the worst, they believed in convictions that explained the reason why events were done the way they were and also how they should respond to situations. The mythology they believed in even provided them with instructions on the way they would interact with one another. Questions like toleration, justice, and punishment were the main reason how they behaved the way they behaved every day.

www.ingramcontent.com/pod-product-compliance
Lightning Source LLC
Chambersburg PA
CBHW070557010526
44118CB00012B/1358